Blessings'

Laura
Chester

Holy Personal

To Ann

Love

Lopez

Ramon de Nance

y Familia

This collection is dedicated

to

Emily Mason Rose

who makes the holy personal

more than anyone I know

Laura Chester

Holy Personal

*Looking for
Small Private
Places of Worship*

**Photographs by
Donna DeMari**

**Foreword by
Thomas Moore**

Indiana University Press
Bloomington & Indianapolis

This book is a publication of

Indiana University Press

601 North Morton Street

Bloomington, Indiana 47404-3797 USA

www.indiana.edu/~iupress

Telephone orders   800-842-6796

Fax orders   812-855-7931

Orders by email   iuporder@indiana.edu

The paper used in this publication meets the minimum
requirements of American National Standard for Information
Sciences—Permanence of Paper for Printed Library
Materials, ANSI Z39.48-1984.

Manufactured in the United States of America

Library of Congress Cataloging-in-Publication Data

Chester, Laura.
        Holy personal : looking for small private places of
    worship / Laura Chester ; photographs by Donna
    DeMari ; foreword by Thomas Moore.
            p.   cm.
        Includes bibliographical references (p.   )
        ISBN 0-253-33804-2 (cl : alk. paper)
        1. Sacred space—United States. 2. Spiritual life.
    3. Chester, Laura. 4. United States—Religion.   I. Title.
    BL2525 .C45 2000
    291.3'5'0973—dc21   00-038288

1   2   3   4   5   05   04   03   02   01   00

CONTENTS

FOREWORD BY THOMAS MOORE

INTRODUCTION

Little Rose Chapel Conceived

When we are seized by the spirit, we may be tempted toward grandiosity. We may become inflated, believing that we know and possess the truth. We may become missionary and zealous as we try to convince the world of our favored beliefs. And we may build huge edifices that proclaim the inhuman scale of our faith. But spirituality leads in another direction when it mixes with our humanity. We care for each other, regardless of our different beliefs, and we house our spirituality in simple shrines and chapels.

I appreciate the humanity in the stories of chapels and lives that Laura Chester has put together in this book. She includes herself, her family and friends, and the people both kindly and belligerent who were part of this episode in her life, in which she built a chapel. She doesn't feign innocence in her tales of spiritual exploration. She admits the full range of her feelings, the full range of her life, and therefore the full range of what it means to make a private place of worship.

Building is always an interior process as well as an exterior one. Just building a house, one wonders exactly what is being accomplished, since emotions run the full scale and difficulties multiply upon each other. This book is about the making of a soul—not just the author's, but that of the people who appear and the reader who is interested. Its episodes of birth, illness, and death are not peripheral to the chapel theme, because the spiritual life cannot be separated from these basic human foundations.

We learn about the fantasies that inspire ordinary people to use colored light, thoughtfully chosen wood, stone, and animated statues to make a microcosm of their beliefs. Angels, spirits, and God find shelter, offer special healing and inspiration. To me this book is a compendium of holy magic, a lost yet vital art for anyone who would take religion out of the attic of intellectualization, down to the earthen floor of felt and meaningful spirituality. Laura's book represents the best way of doing theology—keeping it relentlessly human and thoroughly concrete.

It helps me to have known Laura for many years and to appreciate her passion and sensitivity, to love many of the places she writes about and even some of the people. This too, is the way spiritual writing ought to be—particular but not excessively personal, moving but not excessively sentimental. It doesn't matter if her book inspires other people to build their own chapels; this is not a how-to manual. But I do hope that readers learn how to be spiritual without sacrificing the complex relationships that affect all we do and all we are, acknowledging the role of materials and images that give our spirituality a body. Without that body, we are left with abstract convictions that often lead to conflict. With that body, our spirituality remains low, earthy, loving, and beautiful. The ultimate effect of a worthy spiritual life would be beautiful lives in a beautiful world. This beautiful book is an excellent start.

Introduction

The idea for this book came unexpectedly, almost like being surprised by love when you are not seeking it out. And as with love, I had to follow, see where this pilgrimage would take me, moving from one small sanctuary on to the next, from one radiant story onward. Even at the beginning, I could feel the strands of an ever-expanding network spreading across the country, connecting me to these small bird nests of worship and to the wonderful, spirited people who'd built them.

In February of 1997, I was staying alone on a small ranch near Patagonia, Arizona, working on a novel set in this grand yet desolate wilderness. With coyotes howling in the foothills at night, I had to admit to feeling a bit nervous. Sympathetic to my uneasiness, the owners of the ranch drove their truck out from town to have dinner with me, and invited another couple to join us.

The next-door neighbors, Lori Mendez and Earl Niichel, arrived in a burst of joviality. We all sat around the rustic ranch kitchen laughing and trading stories, eating skillet-grilled trout, roasted potatoes, and a big green salad. Lori and Earl offered their phone number in case anything came up, and urged me to come visit the following day—they were just finishing construction on a hexagonal log home, which they planned to use as a bed and breakfast, and they had also built their own chapel. I was intrigued and asked Lori why she had wanted to build a chapel. She answered simply, "God is so good. We wanted to do something in return."

The next day was Sunday, and I was going to visit St. David's Monastery just north of that great tourist attraction, Tombstone. Hoping for a meditative Lenten experience, I found only a tour bus full of American shoppers. One woman even came to Mass with pink plastic hair curlers in her hair, and another kept tapping her foot so persistently I found myself annoyed. Perhaps on a quieter day I would have had a different experience, but now I felt disgruntled—not my parish, not my priest, not the service I was used to. But perhaps it was more than that—despite the monumental, towering cross by the parking lot, some soul quality was lacking.

The only real conversation I had was with a slightly alarming monk who came sailing up to me after Mass to tell me how hot his robe was, made of polyester. "It's tolerable now," he explained, "but in another couple of months we'll be praying—*Jesu Jesu Jesu.*" I wondered why they didn't make the robes out of cotton. Why did I feel so out of place here? I had hoped to eat lunch with the community, but when I asked, I was told brusquely that I had to make a reservation. Because of the tour they were all sold out.

Driving back to the ranch in the San Rafael Valley, I was relieved to feel the holy silence of that open space, a bit like the silence of underwater, the feeling one gets in meditation when the world drops away and you are left with a sensation of deep repose. This was what I loved about the San Rafael, how there was no interference, no distraction between the human and heavenly realms.

Sitting out on the porch with a cup of afternoon tea, the sun an hour from setting, I realized that if I wanted to see Earl and Lori's chapel, I should go now. Driving down their long, bumpy driveway, I was greeted by seven dogs, friendly curs. Lori and Earl walked back up the driveway with me to *The White Dove of the Mesa.* From the outside it appeared to be a small adobe church in miniature, whitewashed extremely white. I was awestruck by the beauty of its placement, across from a stone-lined park of manzanita, the grounds lovingly tended. Small angels knelt on two post tops at the open gate, which led to vibrant blue doors, and a large oak tree in the courtyard lent cooling protection.

Lori and Earl, who met each other late in life, had designed their chapel together. In contrast to the tourist attraction I'd visited earlier that morning, as soon as I entered here, I could feel, sense, smell, something very special. Rose incense had been burned earlier in the day and it still lingered, mixed in with the scent of rose petals left to dry.

The White Dove of the Mesa, a Rosicrucian temple, acknowledged many of the world's great religions. A small Buddha sat in the left-hand corner, a Tibetan mandala painted above. In different niches around the room, Lori had painted holy symbols—on the right, representing the East, was a depiction of the rising sun, with a medallion of Jesus above five Hindu gurus. On the left, representing the West, she had drawn a picture of the earth caught in an American Indian spider web of illusion, a crab holding the moon in its claws.

Behind the triangular altar, there was a hand-painted nighttime-blue panorama of the San Rafael Valley, with the subtle outline of the Huachuca Mountains, graced by a slender crescent moon. Above that scene in the dark blue sky, Lori had painted a descending dove, wings outspread—an image of the Holy Spirit.

A candle burned before a replica of the Infant of Prague, and above Him, Lori had painted the words PAX PROFUNDIS. She said she had various regal costumes for Him—but He was currently dressed for the Southwest, with a purple robe and deerskin moccasins.

There was something reminiscent of the playhouse here in this small temple. It made me realize that one of the charms of the private chapel is its small scale, which can almost transport one back to childhood. In fact, the smaller the space, the more the imagination is engaged, as if entering the mysteries of the microcosm. Maybe that is the blessing bestowed on children— to be able to find everything in almost nothing.

I am reminded of a phrase from St. Thérèse of Lisieux, *the little way of spiritual childhood.* She taught that "wholehearted imitation of the childhood perfections and virtues of the Christ Child was mankind's easiest road to spiritual perfection." Do we enter the kingdom only by retrieving the insights of that lost innocence? By emptying out and being so open to the present moment that all of creation can be perceived—connecting and therefore glorified?

Children play and worship with such abandon, absorbed in their own immediate world. Perhaps intense play *is* a form of worship, and even playing church can be a kind of practice, just as playing mother or doctor prepares a child for later versions in adult life, though a once-devout friend told me how severely she was punished for pretending to be a priest, placing Necco Wafers on her young friends' tongues. I couldn't resist, and gave her a roll of them for Christmas. We laughed and laughed, while her mother shook her head and said, "You were always so bad."

But that same friend was allowed some of the most inspired Halloween costumes—she got to dress up as Saint Francis of Assisi, with tiny birds sewn to her shoulders. Another time she was Pope Pius XII, and wore a High-Mass altar boy's outfit, with an authentic Pope's cap and huge ring—the whole rig! Now this same friend, Anne Fredericks, makes the most beautiful mirrors— hand-carved, water-gilded, sacred Celtic tree altars that lend a heavenly glow to her darkened hallway. The creative life does not limit itself to a single gesture—it touches all it touches. The creative impulse is the most precious remnant from our spiritual childhood, and it lives on, in wonder.

I think many children have an instinctive desire to create a sacred space, where they can be themselves, undisturbed. Often these homemade constructions are pieced together outside in nature, forts or clubs, but sometimes they are simply made under the bed. Creating one's own private chapel is a bit like throwing a sheet over a card table to make a house. In that simple gesture of draping, a nest is created, a haven, a hideout, something to guard and carefully share.

When I was ten, preparing for my first communion in the Episcopal Church, I made an altar in my bedroom, covering a box with a white cloth, laying out candles and bouquets, keeping various treasures behind this makeshift table—meaningless items to the uninitiated—jumbled together in my pink leather jewelry box. There is a definite need to adorn one's private, holy space, to make it personal. Teenagers do this in their own seemingly unholy way, but all those knickknacks, junky collections, and stubs saved, scribbles recorded on the inside of a closet door, are like stations along the path in life, and to the growing, often suffering, individual, they take on a kind of sacredness. Certainly it is an act of sacrilege for any mother to come in and clean things up.

After a week on the San Rafael, I left Arizona and headed to Baja to meet my son, Ayler, who had been camping out with a group from school on the uninhabited island of Espíritu Santo. I couldn't imagine how a group of teenagers would entertain themselves without any restaurants, music, or media, but on greeting him in La Paz, I had never seen him looking more radiant.

We spent one night in this glorious town, eating heaping portions of seafood in view of the curving waters of the bay, watching young children walking with their families, enjoying the evening sociality. The next morning, in our rented red jeep, we drove the long way to Todos Santos, where we were to visit my friend, the painter Walker Buckner.

Staying at our little *casita* hotel was another artist, Valer Austin, who was also far away from her home in the Chiricahuas. When Walker began teasing me about converting to Catholicism, this perky little woman in her long, blue-jean skirt and laced-up boots leaned over and told me that she had also converted, adding almost in a whisper, "I even built my own chapel."

Raised on the Upper East Side, Valer had moved from the high society of Fisher's Island to the Catholic, Latino culture of southeastern Arizona. With the help of Mexican-Indian builders, she and her husband had constructed a small stone chapel. Using the ancient technique of painting on plaster, Valer had created a fresco around the interior, depicting the creation myth— forces of light and darkness converging behind the altar. How strange, I thought, to have met two people on this short trip who had built their own private chapels.

That night after dinner my son convinced me that he could take our rental jeep and drive off to the beach to meet a new acquaintance. I agreed, but told him I wanted him back before midnight. By four in the morning, I was in a state of panic, sure that he had hit a cow on the road or been swept out to sea, that he was drunk on tequila, or had been dragged into the bushes, robbed, murdered, beaten. Stranded without car or telephone, there was nothing I could do. I lay in bed and wept. But in the midst of my angst, I found myself turning to Mary, asking for comfort, wanting her blue enveloping peacefulness, and finally, I slept.

When I awoke the next morning, I had the title to this book, *Holy Personal,* and there was my son, safe and asleep in his bed. I was grateful, very grateful.

Later that afternoon I drove over to the little town of El Triunfo, and seeing the church by the side of the road, I lifted a rusty wire from a decrepit knob and let myself in. The space inside was cool, and doves fluttered up above as if it were a dovecote. How appropriate, I thought, to hear them cooing, the rustling of their wings in the open rafters. There on the wall, in the frame surrounding a picture of the Virgin Mary, was a tiny photo of a beautiful dark-haired boy, and I wondered what prayer requests his mother had made.

As we sat together later over tea, Valer commiserated with me about the difficulties of raising a teenage son. Looking back, she wished that she had been more strict. I was pleased by her reaction to the idea of the *Holy Personal* book. She knew of a hay-bale chapel in Elgin, Arizona, *La Capilla de San Ignacio,* built by the artist Patsy Lowry, and she urged me to go see it.

I wondered if the Southwest in particular, with its milder climate and expansive geography, lent itself to the small, sacred space. Certainly all over Mexico one saw shrines by the road—spirituality penetrating everyday existence. It was not just a Sunday or someday thing. A corner of even the simplest home was often dedicated to Our Lady of Guadalupe or some other personal saint. Perhaps this Latin influence had spread northward, across the border. Perhaps the spirituality of our own Southwest was throwing its special light toward the darker, colder parts of the country.

I returned home to the Berkshires of Massachusetts, and on Easter morning, opened the *Boston Globe* and saw an article about Boston artist Michael

Dowling, who had created his own sacred space in the root cellar of his home. Everyone I spoke to seemed to know of another small, private chapel—one in the Alabama back country, another on Grand Isle in Lake Champlain, a Norwegian stavkirke in Wisconsin, a Tibetan stupa in Puget Sound.

I began to explore this phenomenon, making one phone call that led to three others, receiving snapshots and encouragement in the mail. I had begun a kind of pilgrimage without a definite map, but I knew if I followed the emerging pattern, I would see some amazing places, and meet many wonderful people with unusual stories to tell.

But I knew this book had to be visual as well as verbal. A new friend, Donna DeMari, a fashion photographer who had worked with many of the top magazines in Europe, had just moved from Paris to South Egremont, Massachusetts. She was still in a state of professional adjustment, and eager to have a new project. Though we knew that religion might not be fashionable, perhaps she could make it so. Beauty was the key, and I knew that Donna of all people would make this a beautiful document.

Meanwhile, I had many questions—what spiritual path led a person to make a private place of worship? Did such a space conflict with or supplement worship in a more public sense? Couldn't one have both? I was curious about how a private sacred space affected a couple's relationship—how did they share their feelings within their chapel—did it nurture a marriage on a deeper level? How was it different when you directed your own sacred space without the counseling advice of a priest, rabbi, minister, or guru? Do most chapels get blessed in some dedication ceremony? Was sacred geometry or any ancient tradition of architecture used? Why do artists often have an impulse to explore the spiritual arts? What is it like to ask a priest or rabbi into one's own *Holy Personal* space? How might he or she react to a place that is so individual?

This book is filled with diversity because this is an American story. Most private chapels in the United States today are not built for show, like the exclusive, grand chapels found on historic estates. Those demonstrations of wealth are often miniature versions of great cathedrals, but rarely do they have the profound personal quality of the more modest examples included here. The small private chapel is built from the heart—"You do it because you feel the need to," one owner said. And sometimes it's nothing more than a chapel built into the closet of a bathroom, that most necessary room for rejuvenation and relaxation, as was Kate Strasberg's *Closet Chapel* in Palo Alto.

In contrast, when my grandparents moved into their house on North Lake Drive in Milwaukee, they found a tiny home chapel facing Lake Michigan, with a beautiful stained-glass window, a miniature altar, and kneeler. But my grandmother, ever expedient, turned the closet chapel into a clothes closet. My father said how he always thought there was something wrong about that, taking a sacred space and making it utilitarian.

But chapels do have their own peculiar lives as they pass from hand to hand. In its heyday the Miller Beer family mansion on Wisconsin Avenue had a fine *biergarten,* subsequently turned into an exquisite chapel with stained-glass windows all around. When I went to visit, ever hopeful, it looked splendid from the outside, with its copper domed roof like a mini-basilica, a beautifully proportioned cross gracing the top. I walked through the old German mansion with its honey-colored wood, each room more sumptuous than the next, decorated to the hilt for Christmas, and was led out to the chapel through the original kitchen, on through a glassed-in walkway, full of anticipation—I was about to see a gem—when suddenly I stopped, spiritually winded, for I was in the middle of a spiritless place of spending, a typical, tacky, Midwestern gift shop. The chapel was no more.

Talking about the *Holy Personal* with me, my husband, Mason Rose, said, "You know, in the early fifties people built bomb shelters. Maybe now they are building chapels." The bomb shelter, that mini-mausoleum, did give the illusion of being a safe space, with a lock as large as a steering wheel, with its cozy bunk beds and cans of food, walls thick enough to deter radiation. But now the thought of entombing one's family in a cement chamber to protect them from nuclear disaster seems more than absurd. The bomb shelter was actually a monument to fear, it held out the false promise of protection, but hopefully we have moved from an era of fear to a time of hope. Death is inevitable—it comes to us all. The creation of a sacred space is not so much a means of finding safety, or of securing oneself from tragedy, any more than it is a guarantee of salvation, but at least the impulse is positive.

Though we may not have to create our own secret, underground chapels because of persecution anymore, there is still a yearning for religious privacy, a deep desire to create for oneself a holy chamber, a place where creative expression joins hands with devotion. We need a place devoted to tranquillity in a world that is always pushing us outward. Here, in these small silent rooms, without distraction, one can sit still, hear the inner voice, give thanks, and be at peace—*Pax Profundis*—before moving on.

Holy Personal

Little Rose Chapel Conceived

When I began thinking about this book and the holy personal in our lives, it seemed natural to consider building our own small chapel. Here it was, Easter Day, a balmy evening—I had just been initiated into the Catholic Church the night before, and now as the sun began to set, Mason suggested that we go out and look for the perfect site.

Mason has lived on Rose Hill for most of his life, and in many ways, for him, I think, this piece of land, with its big mature trees and spacious views, is itself a kind of sanctuary. When he was a child and his parents were building Little Sutton, Mason would climb up to where our house now rests, nestled into the hillside. He'd sit on the large ledges of granite and look at birds hopping about in the shallow pools of water, red-tailed hawks circling above. Even at that early age he enjoyed his own peaceful solitude.

Though Mason is not interested in joining me regularly at church, he seems taken by the idea of building our own small chapel. Soon we are full of imagination, fantasizing away. We walk down the hill past the bluebird box, which he opens with the teeth of his hammer, sweeping out last year's debris, making it ready for its new occupants. Then we check on the beehives, prying up the frames that hold the beeswax. Two mice hop out and run for an open crack in a nearby apple tree. Moths and mites and mice have made a mess of the hives, but soon a new swarm of Italian bees will arrive at the post office, buzzing like mad in their container—it always sends the postal workers into a state of mild panic until we can pick them up.

Hanging the hammer up on a limb, Mason says, "Follow me." We walk down a steep incline to a little spring that is set back in a grove of trees—what do I think of this spot? It is a beautiful, hidden area, but you can see the driveway, and it doesn't feel quite right to have to approach our chapel on such a rugged incline. I want easy access. I want the approach to be private, just distant enough for a sense of seclusion, but pleasurable to get to—no heroic effort—so that we will want to make a visit at least once a day.

Then Mason has another idea. He leads me back up the hill to a special spot at the very edge of our property. Pointing out the nearly indiscernible stone foundation, he tells me that once an old farmer's hut stood here, back when this mountain was open farm country, grazed by milk cows. Perhaps on certain bad-weather days, the farmer from across the valley needed a place of protection.

As a child Mason imagined that there was treasure buried beneath this spot. This magical feeling persists and is contagious. It is a lovely, hidden place, at the end of the birch grove, looking into the forest on one side, out across the high mown field to the west. As the sun begins to sink and dusk lends a transitory glow to the outlines of tree and ridge, we stand on the slightly sunken, leaf-strewn spot, and it feels exactly right.

Being a mover of earth and stone and limbs of trees, Mason immediately begins to visualize how he wants to clear the woods toward the east. We both agree that we would like to have the altar in perfect alignment with the rising sun at the summer solstice. I imagine a triangular window at the topmost corner of this eastern exposure, letting in light that would drop through a shaft, down through an oval opening in the barrel vault above the altar. Perhaps there would also be small stained-glass windows to the south and the north, set back into niches of stone. A heavy chestnut door would form another arch, opening toward the west as an entrance.

On that Easter evening, after a full weekend of family and feasting, we stay up together in the living room, comfortably alone, and draw different plans. Mason has a wonderful, innate sense of space and design. Once we can visualize what we want, we will probably also get the help of Mason's architect brother, Jonathan, who designed our house and barn.

We both agree that we want to build the chapel out of fieldstone from the wall that runs through the woods, no longer containing grazing cows, but still creating a beautiful demarcation. If we are discreet, maybe we can retrieve enough stone and not ruin the look of the old line. The stone would give the small structure a feeling of substance—or would it seem cold and clammy inside? Would spiders and snakes make our chapel their home? How would we keep it heated?

I picture the inside, not dark and cold, but plastered round, very feminine, the curves of the arches giving the space a vaulted effect, making the space inside this small shrine like the inside of one of those fanciful Easter eggs with its delicious interior landscape—a fantastically sweet space capturing light with gold and rose, enveloping. I envision the floor unpolished, tumbled marble. We both are drawn to the Roman arch and want the chapel to suggest the curved, rather than the vertical or angular.

Mason gets out his yellow pad and begins to draw a preliminary plan in the shape of a cross. He imagines that it will have a central altar, with a small extension on either side. It seems splendid, but perhaps a bit too splendid? How much would this cost? Could we do a lot of the work ourselves? In response to that, Mason wonders if it wouldn't be just as good to have an open-air chapel, an intimation of a space with a stone altar and a few benches, a temple out under the trees. But that isn't what I long for—I want to be embraced. We can always take an expansive walk through the woods and contemplate the awesome beauty of nature. A chapel is something different. It holds you and takes you inward.

I realize that I am being drawn back in memory to times when my cousins and I played in our neighbor's playhouse, how it was like entering another world, how we were in charge of that world, and how wonderful and special that was, to create our own drama within ordinary life. There is something about the small space that allows the imagination free rein, perhaps because of the safe feeling of the small container.

I swing back and forth in my mind, imagining an empty, beautifully colored, light-filled prayer place, and then a soulful cluttered repository for all the holy objects and pictures I've collected. I want to embed the bejeweled cross I found in Arizona, made by an Indian woman—it seems full of blessed energy—into the plaster wall above the holy water font. I hope that Father Peter will let me bring holy water from St. Bridget's bubbling well and that he will come and bless our chapel when it is ready to be christened—Little Rose Chapel, in honor of St. Thérèse of Lisieux.

Maybe one of our four children will get married here someday. I wonder what celebrations and memorials will be held within this small space. Having lost a friend this year to cancer, and now facing the illness of my father, I have had death on my mind, ever present, but that awareness also makes me feel the preciousness of life even more keenly.

As Mason and I stand on the crest of the hill and darkness drops slowly down around us, we hear the call of an owl from deep within the forest and feel that this day, the great mystery of the Christian year—Easter—time of resurrection and renewal, has blessed us both with these plans for Little Rose Chapel.

PART ONE

The Pilgrimage Begins, East/Midwest

I come here to find myself.
It is so easy to get lost in the world.

—John Burroughs,
Chapel in the Woods

MICHAEL DOWLING

Root Cellar Chapel

South Boston, Massachusetts

Michael Dowling's spiritual life and creativity both thrive in the same dark instinctual climate. Leading us down the back staircase out into his garden, he shows us a tiny three-and-a-half-foot-high door with a metal brake blade on the front, as if to say—*Stop,* leave your rational mind and worldly concerns outside. Bending low, we enter another realm. In the dim light of underearth, blue votive candles flicker beneath the Stations of the Cross on either side of the room.

At the end of the space, red votives flicker on the brick altar. Here an arched frame taken from a top-floor storm window holds an oil painting of blue-grey sky, cloud and air—a painted lead statue of the ascending Christ hooked to the middle—I have never experienced the Ascension in such a moving, visceral way. White hyacinths from Easter stand on the altar, the cool moist atmosphere of this crypt-like space keeping them fresh and perfumed. Looking closer, I see old newspaper obituaries surrounding the arched frame, lining the sides of the end alcove. A silvery grey wash obscures the print, though the dark ashy columns remain visible.

We turn our attention to the first Station of the Cross, and I realize that these fourteen pieces are abstract. It is an entirely new experience to perceive the Passion in this way—not literalized, but evoked. The paintings are held by similar but slightly different fourteen-inch frames that Michael retrieved and gilded. Most of the material that went into the chapel was either found or given to him. He points out a large glass candleholder, and says that he found it in the trash at a flea market after the vendors left.

7

In the middle of the first Station of the Cross, *Jesus Is Condemned to Death,* hangs a link of chain. Michael holds it in his hand: "I always encourage people to put their hands on these pieces." Our eyes are only now beginning to adjust, and Michael picks up the votive candle from beneath the second station, *Jesus Is Made to Carry the Cross,* which presents a circle of tacks. The moving light makes them appear to be a growing crown of thorns—I touch them with my fingers.

Each of the paintings has a similar palette—earthy reds, dense black, touches of gold. These are dark portraits that make one connect to one's own inner darkness, where only the hidden light glows. The third station, *Jesus Falls for the First Time,* like two of the others in the room, is all red. We move slowly from painting to painting, handling each. He turns one over to show Donna and me the small gilded crosses etched on the back—four crosses marking the fourth station, five for the fifth.

"I did these paintings in 1990 for a show in San Francisco at Grace Cathedral," Michael explains. "They were being installed during Holy Week, and were going to be used as icons. It struck me that I was no longer just making art work, I was making sacred objects that people were going to use for ritual." The paintings were misplaced for a year in San Francisco, but then they reappeared in New York. From New York they got lost again and ended up in Washington D.C., but they mysteriously came back to Michael two summers ago. "A UPS box arrived at my front door, and it was the original box I had packed them in. I guess they had been on their own mission!" he laughs. "So, I opened the box and brought them down here, knowing at that moment this had to be a chapel. The stations seemed absolutely destined for this space." Seven of them hang on either side of the room. "I never really *got* the Passion before," he admits, "but working on this, I realized how personal it could be— how we too take a second and a third fall—how we too witness our mother's grief, and accept the cloth from Veronica." The fourth station is perhaps the most beautiful, a gold etched circle containing a square, where Christ meets his mother. Michael touches this image tenderly. I feel that I should do the same. Two small nails stapled together represent Simon of Cyrene taking up the cross, but in another sense, he feels this station is also about the power of male relationship.

As our eyes continue to adjust to the darkness, the mysteries of the little chapel reveal themselves. The greyish walls and low ceiling make the space very intimate. Michael points out a beautiful round stone in the foundation rocks beneath the brick altar— it is a supporting stone that looks like a massive mill-stone.

Passing a large six-inch rusted nail hung in the middle of the eleventh station, we stop at a golden niche set into the chimney—"The Niche of Innocence," he explains. Here a cherubic angel hangs above the broken hand of an Infant of Prague, who holds a small globe of the world. Candles burn in the interior of this glittering cube, in contrast to the grey limewater wash on the rest of the walls.

Once Michael decided that he wanted to make this space a chapel, he had to add one wall to create the right balance, leaving a very personal *Lady's Chapel* to the left of the entrance. There is an old *prie-dieu* set before this most splendid little altar space that holds an array of family photographs, a few portraits of dogs that have passed away. He holds up a picture of a niece who committed suicide. Today is the anniversary of her death.

On the wall to the left of the *prie-dieu* are various images of St. Thérèse, who rained down roses from heaven. I have brought a little St. Thérèse card with me— *St. Thérèse, The Little Flower, please pick me a Rose from the Heavenly Garden and send it to me with a Message of Love.* I leave it on the ledge beneath a bouquet of dried pink roses hung between various images of the young, beautiful saint. One of the images is so water-damaged it makes her look as if she has been here for decades. The whole chapel has the resonance of something so old it encompasses great reaches of time. A space somewhere between the beauty of candlelight and utter darkness, a place between worlds, half buried, like the realm of the semi-conscious.

I tell him how special St. Thérèse's Church in Patagonia was for me—that I had an important reconciliation there a year ago before Easter. Though I wasn't a Catholic at the time, the priest allowed me to take Holy Communion. Michael goes on to talk about the importance of that word, *reconciliation,* how it is a much better choice than *confession.* He remembers when he was a child, how kids thought they had to make things up in order to have something to confess, so they were really being initiated into lying.

I light a red candle for my father, who will soon be undergoing cancer surgery. Michael takes the candle and places it beneath the central image of Christ on the altar. I know my father would be pleased.

I notice that the little holy water container is empty, and Michael goes outside to find his grandmother's rain-filled bucket. "My grandmother always kept this little glass bottle marked Holy Water"—he shows it to me; the letters are raised, a worn blue—"and she'd fill it right out of the tap. We'd say, 'That's not *real* holy water!' But she'd dab some on her finger and *push* a shoulder for a good God Bless." Michael seems as amused as a young engaging child sharing his secrets in this treasure of a space.

But there's a part of the story of this chapel that's especially curious, he admits. "When I first moved into this house years ago, I could feel a disturbance. It made it very difficult to live here sometimes, but after unearthing the chapel things began to change."

When Michael first noticed the little garden door and pried it open, the room was partially filled with dirt, but he decided it would be an ideal place to hold the anniversary dinner he was planning for his parents, so he swept it out and lined the walls with Mylar. The floor was all poured concrete, except for one corner.

He kneels down to show us a spot where several small candles burn on the floor beside an oyster shell holding a mother-of-pearl cross. "I thought I'd dig this area up and cover it with brick, but as I dug"—he pauses, wondering if he should share this—"I unearthed the bones of an infant." He decided to leave the bones where they were. He had his grandmother's bottle of holy water and did a simple ritual, but when he was about to place a brick over the spot, a powerful blast of energy flung his hand aside, smashing his thumbnail.

Later, when he began opening up the bricked-in chimney for the golden niche, a huge load of soot came barreling down, covering everything in a baptism of darkness. He was blinded and could barely breathe. The cement floor was buried under soot. He likened this "initiation into darkness" to that of Paul, blinded by brightness, how either extremity can bring revelation through the altered state. At the same time, some plug of stopped-up energy was released, and after this experience Michael felt a deep peacefulness in both the chapel and the house.

Another artwork that Michael is currently working on involves a small well house that will be intensely bright inside, gilded with silver leaf. The name of the piece is *Freshwater,* which describes the gem-like quality of stones when they are wet. This piece will be set in a twenty-six-foot-square room at the Danforth Museum in Farmington, and the hut will be sunk into the center of a raft of tiles laid out in a checkerboard pattern, each featuring a different Celtic design, gilded with silver, copper, and gold. A moving current of water will surround the tiled floor in a copper moat, and spotlights will send rippling reflections up against the soot-smeared, obituary-lined walls. He feels the piece is closely connected to the chapel. In fact, everything in his life seems to connect.

"When I was six, I made a pattern of a checkerboard grid, a purple square, then a yellow square with a purple flower. I had no idea of what I was doing, but for some reason I took it to my next-door neighbor's house, Mrs. Strong, and she said, 'Oh that's so beautiful. I'd love to have wallpaper made out of that.' I recently remembered this—for now I'm working on this tile floor piece, and the tiles, it turns out, are based on early Celtic designs that are exactly the same grid as the grid I did when I was six, the sixty-four squares, which is really a checkerboard or chess board, very big in Celtic mythology."

This all happened before the traditional year of reason. At six years old he wasn't aware of how many squares he was making, but by the time he was eight, his art teacher was teaching his class: *The Six Steps to a Perfect Tree.* "So there I was, looking out the window," he recalls. "It was a beautiful fall day. I had my crayons and I was coloring and coloring—but then she held up my drawing and said to the entire class, 'This is the worst tree I've ever seen a child draw.' Unbelievable. But the thing was, I believed it. Suddenly everything was split in two—everything had a right and a left, light and dark, wet and dry, visible and invisible. It was a time of confusion. My intuitive knowledge got put aside, and it's so hard to retrieve that earlier sense of things. I remember showing the bad tree drawing to a little girl across the street, Jane Nicholson. She loved it, so I gave it to her.

"I was in my studio recently, contemplating these tiles for the *Freshwater* piece—and I had a vision of the checkerboard I had painted when I was six years old. That same day my twin nieces invited me to come to their school as a visiting artist. I thought—OK, I'll go and do a tile project with them. I gave them all tiles to paint on, and I told them the story of Mrs. Strong and my chapel.

"Later that afternoon, when I was dropping my nieces off, my sister showed me Mrs. Strong's obituary. We discovered that the wake was being held right around the corner, so we both went, and I was able to tell her children, my childhood friends, this story. We also talked about their mother's pussy willow bush that had been chopped down when they moved away. Then Jane Nicholson showed up. She came walking into the wake carrying a bouquet of pussy willow wands, and she put this beautiful tree-shaped bouquet at the head of the casket. I love that kind of drawstring that pulls various events of your life together."

Michael brings out a cardboard canister of myrrh incense. It looks like little gold pellets. He heats up a piece of charcoal and places it on the brick altar, sprinkling granules of myrrh that fill the room with smoke. "I go heavy on the incense," he laughs. "You can't have enough incense. I get all my religious supplies at this store in Dorcester. I went there this year to buy a bundle of palms for Palm Sunday, and the woman said, 'These are for parishes only,' and I said, 'Oh, I'll just take one bundle then, please.' She didn't know what to say to me, so she just shrugged and rang them up."

Michael burns the palms on Ash Wednesday, igniting the fire right there on the floor, leaving the pile of ashes before the altar during Lent. "I don't put any on my face, but I pick them up with my hands—it has a great deal of sacredness around it. When my nieces come over—they love this little chapel like children do—they say, *Oh we need more ashes!*"

The Easter season is honored through many rituals. "When we have the Holy Thursday dinner down here, it's obvious to me what communion means." Thirteen friends all gather together in community and break bread, reenacting the Last Supper. They bring down a long table and pull up the two benches that rest against either wall.

During Lent all the images of Christ get covered with purple satin, and on Good Friday the altar is stripped bare. Easter morning is a time of flowers and music and re-dedication. Armloads of lilies are carried in, and all of the ornaments return to their rightful places.

I ask him if he doesn't miss taking the Eucharist, and he says that he does sometimes go to his family church in Quincy to take communion. The priest from that church comes to his little chapel once a year to offer Mass in honor of Michael's father, and he brings the Eucharist then.

"But my mother the first time she was here, she sat on this bench and said, 'Gee, you know you wouldn't even need a priest, would you.' It was great coming from my mother, that she could see the sacredness of the space."

May Day brings another celebration with a joyful procession. A group of friends make little garlands of tiny flowers for the statues of Mary. He shows me one small figurine, and her wreath has fallen down around her neck, a dried flower necklace now, but soon it will be May again and she will be freshly adorned.

"And what about Christmas?" I ask. "Do you keep your crèche things handy? Do you think we could set them up?"

"It might be fun," he admits, a bit tentatively, because, after all, it isn't the right time of year, but then he realizes—"You just want to play!" The rough stonework beneath the altar with its ledges and caverns is a perfect setting. He digs out the box, and down on our hands and knees we unwrap each figurine, and trade stories about how much we used to love setting up our childhood crèches. He said how he liked to take Mary and send her flying through the air to Egypt. Even now, absorbed like small serious children, we are both very exact in our placement of each animal, wanting to get it just right. We crowd a flock of sheep on one high ledge beside a kneeling shepherd, placing the wise men coming from the east, arranging the large breathy animals—the cow, the ass—close to the manger, two kneeling angels on the highest crag, and it is an amazing scene, with small blue votive candles set amongst the rocky ledges. The red votive candles flicker on the altar above. Here it all is— the blue lights of Mary, the humble birth scene down amongst the cavernous rocks, and then the blood red lights of the Passion, the painting of the ascension lifting off—the whole story in a single tableau.

I ask him if he ever thinks there might be a time when he won't be as involved with the chapel—what if he had to move?

"If that happens," he responds, "I would leave everything the way it is right now—I wouldn't change anything. I'd just close the chapel up, board it up like a tomb. It would stay sealed, just like that, all of it—" the tiny infant bones, the photographs of family, the mildewing St. Thérèse with her dried pink roses, the ascending Christ covered with a drape of cobweb.

I acknowledge how this little chapel makes one more aware of death, how the darkness comes so close, it makes you draw in breath with a new precious awareness, making you more in touch with the greater mysteries and the personal passion of life.

Amenia, New York Greek Orthodox Chapel

After dropping my son Ayler off at Millbrook School, heading home through Amenia, I notice a small chapel on a craggy hillside by the side of the road. I pull into the driveway. The main house looks like a large Greek temple with huge columns. There is no one around, though I see a pen of llamas, chickens, and a herd of sheep—not your typical country home. I try the next driveway, a more modest farmhouse, all part of the same compound. A man is sweeping the drive, but he doesn't speak English. He goes inside, and a very beautiful woman with a long, black, loosely knit braid approaches my car in black cotton shirt and pants, no shoes. She doesn't speak much English either. I ask her if she is Spanish, and she says, "No, I am Greek," and then yes, of course, her classic Byzantine features come into focus. Her name is Katina Stefanopoulos, and she is married to one of the brothers of Four Brothers Pizza. Suddenly the landscape, the lambs, the Greek temple, all make sense.

I point to the chapel, and ask, "Greek Orthodox?" She nods yes, and motions for me to follow. Above the double door to this white clapboard chapel there are Greek words and a picture of the Sleeping Mary—for as I later learn, they do not believe that Mary really died. They believe that she just went to sleep in her bed.

All four brothers own the chapel together. *Together* is a very important word in the Stefanopoulos family. Katina says shyly that it is such a large family, and they are so constantly together, speaking Greek, that she has not had to learn much English in the ten years that she's lived here. She has mainly stayed home with her two sons, John and Paul, now nine and seven years old.

From the outside, the *Chapel of the Sleeping Mary* looks a bit stark, but on entering, I see a small treasure chest of icons. A red curtain hangs around the altar area, where only men are allowed. Katina crosses herself, bows, and I do too. She turns to a chest of drawers set back in the corner of the room, and gets out a slender white candle, places it in the holder, and lights it. Suddenly I feel overwhelmed. Tomorrow my father has his CAT scan, and I'm afraid of what the results might show. I can feel the sprinkler inside me about to start again, and say, "Can you light one for my father, too?" and then begin to cry, mumbling something about cancer, embarrassed by my display, but Katina understands and says, "Oh, sorry, so sorry."

She is entirely sympathetic, and I feel an impulse of gratitude—I want to thank her for being here, for having this chapel, for inviting me in. She is so beautiful, almost otherworldly. Perhaps because we can't really speak, the understanding between us is sensed more clearly on another level. Before we leave, I lean over and kiss her on the cheek, apologizing for my outburst, but she shakes her head and says with sincerity, "You must come here every day." I tell her that I often drive by on my way to Millbrook, but I live in another state. Her nephew, she says, goes to Millbrook too, and her sister-in-law, Vicky, speaks fluent English.

As I pull away from this small Greek Orthodox chapel, I know what it is that I love about being an American: our all-inclusive ethnicity, for here is a living example of the American dream—a Greek farming family comes over from the little town of Kerteze, and like the proverbial bundle of sticks made strong by holding together, they build up their business, and make a huge success with the best pizza crust in town. The presence of the chapel on this little rise of land must be a constant reminder of their Greek heritage—their religion and values—keeping the family from being swallowed up by the American way, where everything is "just business."

I call Vicky and tell her about my book, and urge her to explain to Katina. I don't want her to think that

15

some grief-stricken lunatic had just pulled into her driveway. I'm leaving for Milwaukee soon to help take care of my father in the hospital. I explain that he is having his esophagus removed, but how we are very lucky, because the cancer was found remarkably early. Hopefully, it has not spread.

My father, still in an upbeat humor, claims that his horse saved his life. Trying to keep up with his young, athletic trainer, he took a long desert ride, and suffered heat prostration. When he couldn't get up, he was taken to a local hospital by helicopter. There they found out that he was anemic, and when more tests were done, they discovered bleeding lesions in his esophagus and then the almost indiscernible tumor, deadly when left undetected for long.

Vicky and I arrange to meet for morning coffee after I return from Wisconsin. I tell her not to make a fuss, but Katina, shy and beautiful as ever, has set a lovely table out on the porch. She has gone all out and made two kinds of cake, one with honey from their home town in Greece. They also bring back their own oregano and olive oil, for as Vicky says, "Olive oil is the essence of the sun and the land. If you buy it here, it's not the same." Even the delicious coffee we are savoring seems to be richer and stronger.

Vicky and her twenty-four-year-old daughter, Elaine, both very elegant, have driven from Rhinebeck to join us. Elaine was named after her eighty-year-old grandmother, who is also present. The elder Elaine does not speak English, but we all sit down together and our conversation flows easily in and out of both languages.

I wonder about such a big family all living in such close proximity—Aren't there conflicts? Don't they ever fight?

"We never do, you know," Vicky answers. "I think it's nice for family to be together. Nice at the holidays too. I like to have a lot of people over in the house, it makes it full of life."

But then I make the mistake of asking about grandmother Elaine's husband, and when she understands the question, she gasps slightly and begins to cry. She lost her husband just a year before. I feel bad for having spoken, and hold out my hand to her as she sniffs back tears. Vicky says, "It's still very hard. No matter how much faith you have, to lose a parent or a child is the hardest thing.

"We buried him in Greece," Vicky explains. "We took his body there because his dream was to be back home." This was a last-minute decision that felt right to the entire family. I ask if he was cremated, but she explains that cremation is against their religion. "He was eighty-five years old, but so much life! Sometimes we'd say—'Oh come on, you old guy,' and he'd say, 'Who's old, not me!' I wish everybody was like him."

They are all genuinely concerned about my father, and I try to give an optimistic report—how the operation was an apparent success, though they did find cancer in one lymph node on the outside of the esophagus, and he will still have to undergo radiation.

When I've talked to my father on the phone recently he has seemed tired, almost depressed, and I have been worried. I tell Katina how grateful I was to visit her chapel during that afternoon of distress, and it comes out that Katina lost her father six months ago. She bows her head and almost starts crying. This could easily turn into a table of weeping women, all dressed in black. Here we are, three generations of women— all of us tending to birth as well as to death, to children and food, to sustenance, survival.

I'm coming to understand that just as with any small animal or infant, a small private chapel needs a primary caregiver, one person in particular to watch over it, in order for the spirit of the place to thrive. It makes sense that Katina would be that person. She lights a candle for her father whenever she can.

Suddenly the phone rings, and it's an international call. Katina comes back onto the porch to tell the elder Elaine that her niece has just died. Elaine gets up to answer the phone, and I can hear the wailing conversation in Greek going halfway around the world, but despite this upsetting hiatus, our conversation continues, as if death itself is part of the normal course of events, linked to ongoing life.

When we go back out to the chapel, the red silk curtains are now pulled back, exposing the magnificent altar with its golden cross, a stained-glass window behind. A strong spring light enlivens the icons, many of them gifts from Greek friends who have visited.

One of the four brothers comes in to say hello. He crosses himself and kisses an icon before he goes off to work. After he leaves, we realize that only a man can light the candles in the altar area, where the women are not allowed. No one seems to mind this tradition. In fact, in Greece, men and women are segregated in church, but here in the *Chapel of the Sleeping Mary,* everyone sits together.

Someone thinks of Paul, who has just gone off with his father to the restaurant. The younger Elaine goes to fetch him, and he returns to put on his silver brocade ceremonial robe. He looks splendid, though he ignites so much incense we have to open the windows.

I have heard that the Greek Orthodox Church is a lot like the Catholic Church, only more so—more ritual, more mystery, more incense. The triangular Eye of God rests at the highest point over the altar, painted by the Amenia artist Peter Wing, who also painted the frontispiece surrounding the altar, as well as the Greek murals that adorn the family restaurants.

Though there are no Aphrodites or Athenas painted here in the chapel, they do appear in the restaurants. I ask Vicky if there are still people who believe in the ancient Greek gods, and she says, "No—that's just mythology." Almost ninety-five percent of the Greek population is Orthodox, and as the young Elaine describes, "In Greece there is a little chapel on top of almost every mountain, and the priest goes from chapel to chapel depending on the name day. Here in America it is the church that helps keep the Greek culture alive. We have Greek school after services, and all the songs are sung in Greek."

It is not a problem that the family does not have a priest every Sunday, though you do have to have a priest for communion. "In our religion," Vicky explains, "a priest is not allowed to have two services in the same day—it has to be a different priest, so it's hard. Sometimes we have friends, priests from Greece who come to see us, and they hold Mass." I suggest that it would be nice if Paul grew up to be a priest, and could lead services in the family chapel. They all agree with their laughter.

Someone mentions that they did have a baptism on the previous Sunday, a son of one of the men who works in the restaurant. The priest is allowed to perform a baptism or a wedding, just not another Holy Communion service. No one knows why. In the Greek Orthodox Church they believe in total immersion, "So you don't want to wait too long, or it's hard to lift the baby!" When Paul was baptized in the *Chapel of the Sleeping Mary,* they had to bring the basin over from the church in Poughkeepsie. The blessed water that is used in the baptism is not thrown out, but poured down a special hole beneath the altar, as if quenching the earth's thirst for souls.

The chapel was dedicated eight years ago, on the day of the biggest feast day of the Greek Orthodox Church, August 15th, which honors the ascension of Mary. "With Mary it is more than a saint. When something happens, the first thing that comes from your mouth is her name. You call her right away—*Please, help me.* Especially for a woman, you feel more close to her, because she was a mother too."

August 15th was also the day of Paul's birth. "Every year he has quite a party! The day before the dedication, Katina was running around, and we said to her, *slow down,* and she said—'Don't worry about me, tomorrow I'm going to be lying in bed, relaxing, and you have to do all the cooking.' And she did it!"

For that first celebration there were about a hundred people and a big tent. Of course not that many could fit into the chapel. They had to stand outside. "In the beginning we were going to make it smaller, really tiny, maybe only for a few people, but then we decided to make it like this, and now we sometimes think we should have made it even bigger."

When I ask Vicky about the difference between going to Mass here in the little chapel compared to the big church in Kingston, she says, "You feel better here. When the priest comes here you feel different—it's almost like the difference between having a baby at home or at the hospital, it's a more intimate, safe feeling." I ask her if she doesn't miss the awesome quality of a big church, and she says, "No, because when you pray, you go inward, and it's almost easier to go inward in a small place."

From Wedding Bells
to a Bavarian Blessing

After only one month of radiation, Dad is down to an all-time low weight. His stomach is now the size of a thimble. No wonder he has lost close to fifty pounds. The entire family is gathering to celebrate his seventy-fifth birthday, and there is a lot of tension in the house. I decide it might be best to get on the road for a few days before the big event. Generous as always, Dad offers us his car, so that Donna and I can have a comfortable road trip. It is luxurious compared to my bottom-of-the-line Escort rental. Heading north on Highway 57, we finally arrive in Waupaca, an idyllic little American town.

Waupaca is set near the Chain-of-Lakes, twenty-two interconnecting, spring-fed lakes that feed into the Crystal River, which flows by Don Schmidt's Old Red Mill, in Little Hope, Wisconsin, just a few miles out of town. Built in 1855, this once-working grist mill handled hundreds of tons of flour in its day, until Don and his parents turned the mill into a rambling colonial-style gift shop. With the help of master craftsmen, they transformed this plain, working mill into a setting suitable for a Currier and Ives picture, building the largest working waterwheel in the state, an authentic covered bridge, and finally a quaint pioneer-style chapel.

Inside the Old Red Mill music plays, and rooms that once held sacks of grain now display cards and statuettes, shelves with every kind of candle, Christmas ornament, and prayer plaque you could possibly want or not want. Don takes me downstairs to the cozy living room that looks out over the Crystal

River, glittering in the morning light. It must be wonderful here in the winter with a fire going, the wind whipping the snow around outside, blanketing the little *Chapel in the Woods.*

When I ask Don why they built their chapel, he admits—"Well, first we built the bridge, then we needed a place to go to." I have to laugh at his candor, but I'm also charmed by the hokey Midwestern quality of the place—two ceramic children sit by the river, watching real children pass by in their rump-bumping inner tubes.

I can see why this is a popular place to get married. The gardens are splendid, and the setting clearly lends itself to this important transition. Even the act of walking through the dark covered bridge over rushing water seems symbolic. "Before it was even done, someone wanted to use it already," Don says. They have had at least five thousand weddings here to date, some with unusual entrances and exits. "One time, some people came down by canoe. They got out of the canoe and had their wedding, and then got back in and went on down river."

Lori Gaedtke and Patrick Turner will be arriving on foot, and marrying first thing this morning. As the two musicians set up outside the little grey chapel that holds eighteen, we help the groom's mother decorate the inside with candles and flowers. "The Queen Anne's lace is from the ditch," she remarks, proud of her economy. With a few ribbons and asparagus fern, it looks quite festive.

The six pews (three on either side), taken from a nearby Methodist church, were cut in half in order to accommodate the intimate dimensions. A window in the shape of a cross brings light to the altar. When the moment arrives, Lori, in her long satin gown, is escorted from the other side of the river to her waiting groom. The family crowds into the chapel, and the overflow huddles by the door. When the bride falters with her vows, moved by emotion, it also brings tears to my eyes.

Marc and Kim Simon are there with a cage of "love birds." They explain how the releasing of doves is an Old World custom, a symbol of peace, love, and prosperity. It can also be seen as a blessing from the Holy Spirit, bestowing serenity and compassion upon the couple. When they open the birds' cage—it is a magnificent sight, this rush of white wings shooting up into the sky above the chapel.

After the ceremony, Donna and I drive on toward Manawa, alerted to the Bavarian Farm Village by a huge privet hedge that is cut into monumental letters spelling out PEACE across a gradual slope. Above the hedge, on top of the rise, is *St. Nicholaus Kirche,* a small replica of the Austrian church where "Silent Night" was first played in 1818.

As we park, two tractors are mowing the field across the road, and the smell of cut hay is ripe in the noontime heat. There is a feeling of festivity, for today the Fergs are celebrating their family's one hundredth year on this land. The farmstead, once a working cow farm, is now decorated to the hilt in Alpine style to give the feeling of a Bavarian village right here in central Wisconsin, where so many Swiss and Germans originally settled and where their descendants continue to live. Even a storage tank is painted with faux stones, and the outbuildings are trimmed with gingerbread, lending a fairytale feel. "This is a farm recycled," Shirley says. "Under our gift shop is where we used to harrow hogs."

The local community has come decked out in lederhosen, dirndls, and Tyrolean hats for the Oktoberfest celebration that has just begun—three months early, but what the heck. There are even T-shirts for sale that imitate the traditional halter straps. I buy a couple for my beer-drinking brothers, a little edelweiss flower pendant for a niece. There are cuckoo clocks and music boxes amongst the European imports and local crafts. Growing up in Milwaukee, I acquired a taste for this brand of *gemütlichkeit,* but it is slightly off-putting to Donna, who has never tasted a bratwurst before, or savored bacon-sweet German potato salad with a mug of dark ale. Some of the men are buying pitcher-sized cardboard containers of brew. It is only lunchtime, and this feast will go on until after midnight. I wish we could witness the state of the *glockenspiel* at that hour.

We are just in time for the renewal of the vows that will take place outside the onion-domed chapel. About forty couples gather by the entrance, and one woman speculates merrily, "You can tell who is really happily married—they're here!"

Reverend Eugene Gauerke begins with an invocation and prayer, then goes on to say how weddings have always been times of joy and celebration.

"This was true in October of 1810, when King Ludvig the second of Bavaria and his beautiful princess were married. The wedding celebration was such a happy event, the king thought it would be a good idea to celebrate it every year, and it became known as Oktoberfest. I'm grateful that the Fergs are reminding us that Oktoberfest means more than drinking beer," the Reverend says. "It began because of a happy marriage. By the way, the Fergs have been married since August 11th. Not this year though." Everybody laughs on cue. "All joking aside, it's good to remember our wedding day, when love was at its best, when nothing seemed impossible, and when joy and happiness and optimism reigned."

Reverend Gauerke leads the couples in the marriage reaffirmation—*Renew our love. Renew our joy in each other. Remind us to take time for what is important. Remind us to do the little things that mean so much. Teach us how to live constructively and lovingly. Help us to praise and uplift each other, building up all that is good. Above all, O God, help us to keep you in the center of our relationship.* Then he closes the ceremony by saying, "Husbands, you can now kiss your brides, or anybody else near you!"

Accordion music comes over the loudspeaker, and soon the *oom-pah* band is warming up. Folk dancing with the *Schuhplattlers* will continue on into the evening. I wish we could stay, but we only have time to share a little apple strudel with Richard and Bernice Dust, owners of a rough-hewn corn crib chapel. They have driven all the way across the state for this event. Richard is a lay preacher who has led worship at almost every church within twenty-five miles of home. Almost shouting over the festive music, he says, "At our own little chapel we don't hear any preaching, cause I don't do any preaching to myself!"

Many Walloon-speaking Belgians still live in the northeastern portion of Door County, preserving this gorgeous farmland as well as their Old World traditions. Following vague directions, we search for the first of several miniature chapels, and feel like we're on some sort of spiritual treasure hunt. Luckily, I take the right turns and stop in front of a tiny white-washed chapel, with a

handmade stone cross set into the masonry above the door. Joe Destree, the builder, was a renowned stonemason, who went blind when he got lime in his eyes. He vowed that if his eyesight ever returned, he would build a chapel, and so he did, dedicating it to St. Adele, the patron saint of sight.

The entrance latches with a simple hook, allowing easy entry. These shrines are so small, shed-sized, that it would be easy to drive right past without even noticing them. This one has a fairly unadorned look. I light a votive candle, sign the guest book left out to record the passing of visitors, and read:

Dear God—Thank you for giving me life and happiness. I love you and your Sun Jesus alot.

*

I believe there is a God and it is brought into each culture in the appropriate way. I have a lot of questions about our religion. I have found through other religions I have gained answers about our own.

*

Dear God, I am devoid of spirituality—an empty shell of a man. Help me to find my anchor—to place myself on the correct path—all I ask is for understanding and guidance.

*

Please help me and my mom to find the strength to quit smoking.

I notice a broken cigarette butt on the altar. Somehow, I suspect that these cries for help would soften God's heart the most, for it seems that when we are truly in need, at the bottom, calling out, He and Our Lady listen, that they rejoice at being able to answer our most humble requests. I write my own prayer request for family harmony and for my father's health, shocked to see that someone has written in big bold letters: MARY IS DEAD. Beneath it I write, *Untrue.*

Driving on to Dykesville, we find the Bader Chapel, dedicated to St. Thérèse. The door is so badly swollen, we have to force our entrance. Inside, I find my happy favorite, her statues and pictures amidst the nubs of old candles and peeling yellow paint. The original owners of this little shrine have probably passed away, for the woman in the new house down the road says the shrine was there when they bought the land, but that she knows nothing about it. The old world and the new.

In the town of Tonet on County K, we find the shrine of the Delveaux family. Their farm is immaculate. Other pristine farms lie here and there as far as the eye can see, every barn and house perfectly maintained. This chapel was built in the 1800s by Mr. Pinlot, a carpenter, who was making ice out on the bay. He fell in, and feared he was drowning; he vowed that if he was saved, he would build a chapel in honor of the Blessed Mother.

It seems that her presence is hovering over this graceful, abundant farm-land, allowing the fields to thrive, and the families to prosper, Mother of the Earth, Mother of the World, Mother of the Son of Man. I feel that I am seeing a whole new side to my home state. It is wonderful being out on the road on this incredible, mysterious journey.

That night after dinner, we share a piece of the most exquisite cherry pie, just out of the oven, with freshly picked Door County cherries baked in a crumbly butter crust, the sweet and sour elements combining to perfection. I am in heaven. Door County is one of my favorite personal holy spots, with its sparkling air, pure water, and smooth meditative stones. Once we reach the Boyntons' charming Scandinavian studio next to *Bjorklunden Chapel,* I too feel like a water-tumbled stone that has found its shore, close to the lapping waters of Lake Michigan.

Door County, Wisconsin # A Scandinavian Stavkirke

I first learned about the Boyntons' sanctuary of peace through a rare first edition published in 1953, *Faith Builds a Chapel,* and was delighted by every detail of the architectural design, purely cruciform, inspired by an ancient stavkirke that stood beside a lake in Lillehammer, Norway, its reflection mirrored in the quiet waters. Winifred Boynton carried this image of tranquillity home, wanting to build her own American version on the shores of Lake Michigan.

Her book is filled with stories about the ongoing creation of the chapel— the squat little whimsical bear cub carvings that guarded the great door, the rough-cut redwood planks that they tried to paint and then had to bleach to lighten the color, the diamond-shaped cedar shakes for the roof, the friendly neighbors who stopped by to help—Mrs. Peil, with her heavy German accent, bringing perennials to decorate the chapel garden. Winifred even molded the wooden threshold, so that it looked like centuries of passing feet had hollowed it out. Hallowed.

In the early eleventh century, the carved wooden stavkirke marked the coming of Christianity to Norway—the beginning of a new era "where a religion based on love would lift man above the darkness of paganism." Unafraid of the barbaric ancestors that inspired so much Scandinavian art, the Boyntons created intricate carvings based on traditional Scandinavian symbols—biting beasts with twisting bodies turning in interlocking patterns, dragon faces that could scare away evil; but primarily, the interior murals were inspired by the message of love from the Gospels.

26

"The part that is most amazing," she wrote, "is that I ever had the courage to begin at all, having so little previous experience or knowledge on which to rely. There was a definite feeling that I, myself, was really *not* doing it. I was merely the small point of the needle placed on the record."

At the end of each summer, husband and wife returned to Highland Park, Illinois, for the winter, but work on the chapel continued. Over the next nine years, in their winter basement they carved together, making the altar, the pew ends, and the baptismal font. When summer came, Winifred would set up her scaffolding and continue painting her glowing earth-toned murals.

Winifred had survived a number of personal family tragedies, and had reached a place that she described as "a complete spiritual vacuum," but out of this dark night of the soul sprang beauty. She came to understand that she was not building the chapel so much as the chapel was creating her. She was pouring heart and soul into the work, but the chapel was returning even more.

Don Boynton admitted, "At first the chapel was a purely selfish thing, a place where I could relax over a hobby, but it finally became—and don't ask me how—a vehicle through which I came to know myself. This chapel represents to me my conviction that people must have a daily spiritual life or they have no Christianity at all."

In the midst of their absorbing work came the shattering news of Pearl Harbor. At least there must have been some comfort in the thought that they were building something beautiful in a world prone to destruction. Peace was the central and unifying theme essential to every aspect of their chapel, for they both felt that there must be a consciousness of peace within before it could be found in the world. Far removed from the confusion and aggression of war, this sacred space became a true sanctuary. "It is so small, so intimate; God is so near He can hear the faintest whisper of prayer. Prayer is the life of the chapel, and as you pause on the threshold there is a spiritual sense of peace, a complete harmony within."

We wake to a Wisconsin kind of day—just the kind of morning I always look forward to after a long stretch of heat and humidity. Set amongst pine and birch trees, with only the sound of bird calls and the gentle, lapping water, the little wooden stavkirke is empty when I enter, and I'm embraced by a feeling of serenity—the dark wood, the subtle blue tones of the stained glass, like transparent jewels, the warm enveloping colors of the murals. It is as intimate as the enclosing arms of a grandmother, and it brings me close to tears.

I think about my father, soon to be seventy-five, halfway through his radiation treatment, but he still maintains such a strength of spirit and good cheer, determined that he is going to live another decade, despite the nausea and exhaustion he's fighting. I sit in a little pew on the left and pray for him and my mother, for my husband and sons. Before me I see the hand-carved cross, the keynote of the chapel. I am drawn to it, and moving forward, I see that the cross does not depict Christ nailed and suffering, but a lovely angel soaring upward, as if asleep, with folded hands, wings outspread.

Winifred was nervous that people might disapprove of this design, placing an angel on the cross instead of Christ. But one day a minister came to visit the chapel—he had lost a son in the war, and he stood before the cross for so long, she had to ask him if the image disturbed him, and he said, "On the contrary, it is a most beautiful interpretation. To me it represents victory over death."

I have to keep this response in mind as I contemplate my father's illness. And to realize again and again that this ultimate victory over death has been offered to each one of us. Perhaps faith and fear do not walk well together, for we are still human and we fear for ourselves, fear that we'll lose the ones we love. Mrs. Boynton certainly must have feared for her sons overseas during the war. Looking up, I see a mural of the Angels of Prayer, beneath a celestial blue ceiling of stars. How those angels must have rejoiced during the Victory Service at *Bjorklunden Chapel* held on August 26, 1945.

Carl, the eldest son, returned home engaged to a French Catholic girl, and the couple wanted to hold their ceremony in the family chapel. Carl wrote to his parents:

> Daily I have become more appreciative of the teamwork and togetherness behind the work you two have done. The very fact of your consecrated work on the Chapel means that you want God to have a hand in your marriage. It is as difficult to put into words what the Chapel means to me as it is to express the depth of my love for you both. I am fully conscious of how much the Chapel is an expression of your faith and how truly it gives evidence to the constructive force of religion working itself out through your hearts and hands. Andrée and I believe that the Chapel will give a special blessing to our marriage, symbolizing as it does the union of all those having sincere love and faith no matter of what nationality or religion.

How true these words must have felt to his parents, for their earliest conception had always been to make a sanctuary that represented all nations and creeds. Even in the earliest stages of building, four German craftsmen, two Belgians, and one Bulgarian all joined together to work with the Boyntons, each taking pride in his individual craft, whether spreading plaster or fashioning the massive metal bands that extend across the entrance door.

"It seemed to us that this little sanctuary of peace would be incomplete without a panel expressing the ultimate hope for world unity. *Let the heavens be glad, and let the earth rejoice.*" Within the design of leaves surrounding the entrance, symbols of many world religions were carved—a lotus flower, a six-pointed star, the American Indian swastika, but above all, the symbol of the world in the hand of God.

With Carl and Andrée's wedding, the life of the completed chapel was now fulfilled. And what a glorious wedding by all accounts—with tall white candles on top of the carved pew-ends, each candle held in place by cedar and spruce, ropes of greenery forming a bower for the bridal couple.

As the years went by, the Boyntons participated in the christening of six grandchildren, baptized in the chapel font they had carved—the work on this single piece alone had taken over six hundred hours to complete. The intricate woodwork illustrates scenes from the life of each Apostle. Sunday vespers in the candle-lit chapel also became a tradition, as did the Swedish mid-summer feast with square dancing and a full smorgasbord, the deep tones of the bell ringing at midnight to bring in the Sabbath. "Voices were hushed as we turned toward the Chapel. Little lanterns edging the path flickered in the darkness. Through the open door the light of the candles streamed out to meet us as we drew near."

This summer picture brings back my childhood, rich with the ethnic heritage of Wisconsin that combines so many European cultures. I feel the closeness of family supporting each other. I see the lightning bugs pulsing and inhale the smell of home—verdant, fecund, water and earth, the evening humidity that is so luxurious and kind to the skin. Soon I will return to Oconomowoc, and we will all join together to honor the oldest member of our growing tribe, my beloved father.

Winifred Boynton has passed away, but her words are present within me—"For our family the day begins and ends in the Chapel. In all our activities there is the consciousness of the hovering presence of the Chapel . . . indeed this has been true ever since the Chapel became a part of *Bjorklunden.* It has shared in everything we did; not as a restraining influence, but as a participating one. . . . We say The Chapel is finished, but we know that the Chapel will never be finished, for it lives, it speaks, it even sings."

JANET WILLIAMS

Adirondack-Style Chapel Lake Champlain, Vermont

Catching the ferry in Plattsburgh, New York, we have an easy twelve-minute ride to Grand Isle, and then a short drive up West Shore Road. A long cedar-lined driveway guides us down to "Westerly," where a stretch of summer cottages cover 1,200 feet of lake front, the lulling waters of Lake Champlain only yards away. We are greeted by Janet Williams and her daughter, Gretchen, as well as by a boisterous golden Lab. Soon cousins and in-laws gather, eager to share their history. Indeed, today it is rare to find a family that has managed to keep a summer place together for six generations.

In 1903, when this land was purchased for a mere $300, the Gemont Graves family camped out along the banks of the lake before building on the six divided lots, designating a certain amount of land "common property." In the beginning, the family came together not only for Morning Prayer, but to share three meals a day. There is still an open-air pavilion where members gathered to sing at night, as well as a tennis court, and a boathouse that has been turned into a bunkhouse where Donna will sleep. I get the screen-sided Coleman trailer, a mobile tent.

Tents are part of the tradition here. The first was named "Wedding Bells Tent," purchased with a savings account accumulated from Rev. John Henry's wedding fees, and later replaced by "Wedding Bells Bungalow," the most gracious home of the lot, with a dark-brown-stained wooden interior that the cousins are reluctant to change. In fact, little has been renovated here, though the family no longer relies on hand-pumped lake water.

31

The real gem of "Westerly" is *The Lady Chapel,* an Adirondack-style construction made out of cedar logs, in keeping with the rustic quality of the area. Attached to the back of the chapel is a high fieldstone cloister garden that extends the dimensions of the interior and creates an overflow space, often used for weddings and christenings. Three cedar trees grow in the corners of the cloister, and Janet remembers the entire area often covered with soft cedar fronds.

Stepping inside, we are immediately taken by the bentwood details curving above, the hand-fashioned altar rail. All of the cedar work was done by an old French Canadian caretaker, Julius Bluto, who watched over the place for years. Despite the casual, rustic nature of "Westerly," this is a high Episcopalian chapel, with polished silver sanctus bell, chalice, and ciborium. Janet assures me that Episcopalians are simply Catholics who can't read Latin. "They flunk Latin!" But I can tell they were raised to know the difference.

The candlesticks for the high altar are made out of birch wood, and with all the candles lit, the chapel comes to life. Even the sun decides to break through the afternoon cloud cover. Streaming through the diamond-shaped windows, it wobbles on the altar, lighting up the red handmade kneelers piled by the rail. Janet pulls the rope to the bell up above, while Cousin Elsie tells me, "It's a proper farm bell, purchased from Sears and Roebuck. I think it adds a lot of class to the place."

The Reverend John Henry Hopkins, grandson to the first Bishop of Vermont, wrote that the chapel was a true haven for him. There was no electricity in those days, and evening services were held by candlelight.

> I preached at each mid-morning service, as a rule, unless some visiting Bishop or Priest were willing so to do, and there was usually an offering, which was always devoted to missionary or charitable purposes. Baptisms were administered, marriage was solemnized, and alas! Burials were held from our chapel, all of which were reported through St. Paul's Church, in Burlington, as the chapel was a purely private and family affair, and not organized as a mission of the diocese of Vermont. The little building was always open all

day long, during the summers, and nearly every day some visitors would pause in their motoring, and would drop in to see it, and to admire its beauty and the seclusion and attractions of the cloistered yard.

Today the family is a bit more reclusive, limiting visits to Sunday services in August. Local gossips like to say that the Graves clan is some sort of "religious cult." The present family members find this hilarious, appreciating the notoriety.

Walking back to Janet's cabin, we remark on the mildness of the air— the weather is balmy, pussy-willow soft. Back inside, Janet pulls out an old black leather photo album with fading prints, where young men hold up strings of fish, and boys are pictured in homemade box boats, playing Indian in costume. Women relatives in long dresses file into *The Lady Chapel,* whose hand-fashioned pergola was laden with grapevines. The chapel was dedicated to the Virgin Mary, but named in memory of Marie, the family matriarch, who died before the chapel was completed.

In the earlier part of the century, the chapel looked as if it were set on prairie farmland, but nature has encroached over the decades. Nature has also pruned, for last winter an ice storm took out numerous trees. Some family members think that even more should be taken down to let in more light, returning the chapel to its original openness, but I rather like the dark cozy feeling the cedars create, as if wanting to huddle around it.

Gretchen, twenty-three years old, has Down's Syndrome. She is very warm-hearted, and gives more hugs in a day than most of us get in a lifetime. Gretchen is particularly interested in the more recent color snapshots of family she can recognize, including herself. She calls Janet "Mother Darling," as if imitating the tone of her great-grandparents, for as the story goes— "Uncle John Henry and Aunt Marie were quite de-

voted to each other, but one time they were out in their rowboat, which they liked to do, taking a little row at night, and they were coming back to shore, and she would direct him, '*To the right, Beloved. To the left, Beloved. To the right, Beloved, to the left,*' until crunch, he hit the pier head on. But there was never an unkind word said, ever."

"Not like we do today," I add.

"Oh, quite different. We got bad mouths."

I am glad that Janet is not overly pious, and she is grateful that we are not church mice. I want to hear all their stories, and there are plenty of those. Sitting around a delicious New England boiled supper, Janet tells us how strict their upbringing was, how the women all wore little white head-coverings whenever they entered the chapel. When I ask if they were ever tempted to play in the chapel as children, they look at me in horror—"*Play* in the chapel? God forbid! We would have been skinned alive."

By the time we are ready for bed, lightning is illuminating New York State across the water, and the sky is electric. The full moon is still under cloud cover, but we know she is there. Unzipping the plastic protectors that cover the screens, I spread out on the queen-size foam mattress. Momentarily I worry about lightning hitting the camper, as rain begins to pelt the roof, but soon I am sound asleep, and when I wake the next morning, the storm has passed. I look out toward the water and see the full moon sinking down into the lake—and in the east, the sun is just beginning to rise through the cedar trees, streaking across the lawn.

Little Audrey Santo's
Garage Chapel
Worcester,
Massachusetts

I am constantly amazed by the wonderful people who have been placed in our path. As I begin to plan a future trip, a series of phone calls leads me to a young black couple in Destrehan, Louisiana, Cheryl and Barras Cloudet. I talk to Cheryl easily for a while, but it soon comes out that last year she lost a son in an automobile accident, and she has been grieving terribly. Struggling to remain composed, she admits how close she was to this boy. Her pain is transferred over the line to me, as if I had touched an electric wire that stretched from her heart to mine. I feel that no matter what I say, it will be horribly inadequate, but ours is a strange and immediate intimacy, and I think she can tell that my heart goes out to her.

Cheryl wants to make sure that I understand that theirs is not a fancy chapel, but rather a simple altar space in their den where they say the rosary with friends every week. I tell her that most of the chapels we are looking at are quite modest. "Day after tomorrow," I add, "I'll be visiting a chapel in Worcester that was made in a one-car garage."

"You mean little Audrey's?" she responds, and I am astounded. Yes, I am going to the home of Audrey Santo. How did she know about that? Cheryl says that last summer, after the death of their son, she and her husband drove all the way from Louisiana to Worcester, Massachusetts, to visit the chapel. This is too strange.

She goes on to say that they were not able to see little Audrey because they did not have an appointment. Only a very limited number of people

are included in the afternoon Masses held every Tuesday, Wednesday, and Thursday.

When I called there, months ago, I mentioned that I was working on a book on small private chapels, and the woman I spoke to tried to put me off, saying that there were very few openings, but I said I didn't mind waiting. She responded by saying that there would only be space enough for one person, so Donna could not accompany me. But I accepted the date, and now, months later, it struck me as very odd that I would connect with Cheryl Cloudet two days before going to the Santos'.

Cheryl says that even though she did not see Audrey, they were allowed into the garage chapel for a few minutes, and given a cotton ball saturated with the holy oil that has been miraculously dripping from pictures and statues for the past several years. Cheryl says that Barras was praying in the corner of the garage and could feel a presence above him, as if there were a hand on his head. He believed it was the presence of the Holy Spirit. But in the middle of his prayers, a woman appeared in the doorway and announced that it was time for them to go.

I am resolved to take a prayer petition to little Audrey for Cheryl and her husband, in memory of their son. Perhaps that is the reason for my visit.

Leaving for Worcester early in the morning, I stop by a florist to buy a Stargazer lily. It is open and fragrant. I want to get to Worcester with an hour to spare, but as I approach the exit and look at my map, I am disconcerted, for the verbal directions I was given over the phone are not terribly clear, and Worcester is a confusing city. I drive up and down Route 122 looking for South Flagg Street, growing more and more anxious as my extra time diminishes.

Finally, after asking for directions several times, I find the right house, but I am told that I cannot park on the street, but have to drive to the local church, where there is a shuttle back to the house. By the time I return, the garage chapel is crowded, and I stand at the very rear. My Stargazer lily is taken inside to little Audrey, while a woman up by the altar leads a tour of miracles, pointing out various pictures that have dripped with holy oil. She motions to one metal cross that is dripping with oil right now, and displays the holy oil that is filling a chalice. She says that various statues in the chapel have bled and wept. Some occasionally move to face the Holy Eucharist un-aided by any human hand.

The Catholic Church, wary of hoax, has had the oil tested in a specialty lab in California. Some of it appeared to be olive oil, while another sample was scientifically designated "oil of unknown origin." A woven image of Christ's Sacred Heart hangs on the wall behind me. It has dripped oil down onto a picture of the Last Supper, spreading into the shape of a perfect chalice. Even more strange and miraculous are the Hosts that have bled on four different occasions. Each is contained in an elaborate reliquary.

A few years ago while a video was being made of the weekly Mass, a priest held up the host to consecrate it, and it began to bleed before everybody's eyes. The cameraman apparently was so moved that he began to cry, while the priest made a motion for everyone to be quiet. *Very very quiet.*

I am amazed that I am even here. There is obviously something super-natural going on in this modest little home in this predominantly Jewish neigh-borhood.

I put Mason's camera and tripod down in the corner. In groups of ten we are invited to go back outside, and then we file into the main body of the house and are led to an anteroom where we can look through plate glass into Audrey's bedroom. There she lies, with her head to the side, her long dark hair streaming down, surrounded by various religious statues and girlish memorabilia, a heart pillow, decorative ribbons and cards. Her own Holy Tab-ernacle rests by her bed. Her mother, Linda Santo, gives her a small portion of the Host every day. It is said that in the ten years that Audrey has been immobile, she has never suffered a bedsore. That alone is inexplicable. I hand over my prayer petition for Cheryl and Barras Cloudet, as well as one for my father.

Back in the garage chapel, Mass begins, led by a frail eighty-year-old priest who has been one of the spiritual advisors to the family for years now. Instead of using wine, the priest puts the Hosts for Holy Communion into the oil that has collected in the chalice. I am the next to last person to receive, and my Host is saturated with the viscous-looking oil at the bottom of the cup, and I worry that it will make me nauseated. I wonder if I am worthy to partake. I can only think that I am here because I will write about this and more people will know about these mysterious signs of Christ's love coming through this helpless victim soul.

Audrey was three years old when she drowned in the family pool. She was resuscitated, but medication left her in a waking coma. Could it be pure coincidence that her accident occurred on August 9th, at 11:03 A.M., the exact time the bomb was dropped on Nagasaki? The family's trials and blessings have been endless since that day.

Nine years ago, Linda Santo took her immobilized four-year-old to Medjugorje, where she was allowed into the apparition chamber of the church with one of the visionaries. Since that trip, the Santo family has gradually come to realize that something very special is going on in their home. Supernatural love has surrounded their daughter, who not only suffers the Passion during Lent, and receives the stigmata and crown of thorns on her forehead, like other historically revered saints, but also seems to take on the symptoms and diseases of other people. Many miraculous healings have occurred.

Audrey's legs have at times taken on the burnt look of someone suffering from excess chemotherapy. Cancer patients who visit here continue to be healed. Another woman was "slain in the spirit" outside Audrey's room, and had an instantaneous recovery from multiple sclerosis just as Audrey went into a spasm that seemed to be a symptomatic transference.

Though the Catholic Church has not yet given their sanction, it looks as if the people are deciding for themselves, coming to Audrey's annual August 9th Mass at Christ the King Church in greater and greater numbers. Last year, eight thousand people arrived, and this year they anticipate an even larger crowd.

Amongst those present now, there is only awe, no worrying over the validity or mystery of what is happening around us. The metal cross on the altar does seem to be oozing oil. I crouch down and see tears streaming from a small stone angel set on the bright blue carpet.

After receiving Communion, we take turns going forward to kiss a reliquary that contains one of the miraculous Hosts, and as I kiss it, I feel a cool, almost aromatic, balsam-like sensation that leaves my lips feeling tingly. Then as I walk past a poster of Our Lady of Medjugorje, her visage streaked from a previous outpouring of oil, the poster falls forward toward me, and I catch her. It's as if she wanted to fall into my arms, or possibly hit me on the head.

I can't help but wonder, why Worcester of all places—this rather ugly eastern city, in this grim northern climate, in this plain, middle-class home, in this rather ordinary neighborhood? There are no exceptionally beautiful icons on the walls. These are factory-made statues, machine-made posters, not hand-painted works of art, and yet they are bleeding, weeping tears, and oozing holy oil. Though I am not a photographer, I think I should try to record it.

Others around me are snapping photographs, and one man is using his camcorder. So after Mass is over, when people are milling about, I set up the tripod and begin taking pictures with Mason's Nikon. I seem to be having trouble with the lens. It doesn't want to move in or out, stuck. I don't know how these pictures will turn out with this minimal light, but I figure I might as well try, though no photograph would convey the supernatural feeling in this place. It is a bit awkward trying to take pictures with so many people tripping about, but I continue until the woman who was leading the tour approaches me and asks, "You aren't from the newspaper are you?"

I say no, but go on to explain about my book, as I had on the phone months ago.

She is horrified, and lights into me, accusing—"This isn't right! You come into a private home and don't ask permission. You have to get permission from the Bishop to take pictures for a book."

Feeling a bit defensive, I point out that everybody else is taking photographs, but she says that those are only keepsakes, and I have brought in professional equipment—it's an invasion of the family's privacy.

I tell her that I am not a professional photographer, far from it, but she is not satisfied. I put my hand on her arm and say, "I promise you, I will not use any of these photographs without getting written permission," but she continues, chastising me. At this point, I ask, incredulous, "Don't you believe me? If you can't believe me, you can have my film." I open the camera, pop out the roll of film and hand it over. There are still other people in the room, and I feel shamed by her accusations. She looks suspiciously at my silver Mexican cross, as if it came from some weird cult, not the customary gold medal hanging around my neck. I can only think that this kind of suspicion cuts and divides, fear begetting more fear, but she is only doing her job, as she says, while I am trying to do mine.

Little Rose Chapel Breaks Ground

Mason and I go out to the site with a shovel and turn the sod in the center of the positioned stakes, ten feet wide, sixteen feet long, though the interior of the chapel will only be 8 × 13, the dimensions of the golden mean.

Everything is going so quickly. I call Bill Warner, the excavator, and two days later his son arrives to dig the hole. His machine has trouble moving an enormous rock that is at the center of our building site. Bill has to come back with an even bigger machine that picks up the six-ton granite rock with its monstrous pincers.

Lou Sartori measures the foundation, and days later he is ready to pour. The cement truck arrives and shoots its sloppy mix down a metal trough into the rectangular footing, burying my sacred bundle, filled with photographs of family, a prayer card for St. Thérèse, a picture of Our Lady of Guadalupe, a new razor blade, a chestnut from Nashotah's leg, a palm frond made into a cross from last Palm Sunday, an amber cross, a jewel from Mason, a little red barn from godson Alden, an earring from Ayler, an iron honey bee, a pin of a cathedral floor plan, a bleeding heart plucked from the bush and a fairy rosebud, my pug dog's hair, an amethyst crystal in an old heart-shaped music box Bunny Kirchner gave me— I listen to it play for the last time—a ruffed grouse feather, a unicorn from my friend Stella, a rose-shaped beeswax candle, a turkey egg, a flattened penny and a pussy willow sprig, Ayler's old ID bracelet, Rosa Venus soap from Mexico, and a calla lily pin from Summer Brenner, all wrapped together in a bright green scarf before I lower it in, forever.

As the cement dries we inscribe the word PAX with our initials, LCC and MCC, on either side, and then the initials of our parents beneath ours, GMC & MSC, MCR & EMR, and then those of our children and brothers and sister, friends, godchildren, nieces and nephews. God Bless Little Rose Chapel written out at the end. Mason wonders what the workmen will think, but I believe they like being a part of this, knowing something unusual is going on. They're glad to have a hand in it.

The cement needs to go down four feet beneath the frost line so that the stone walls above won't be disturbed by the shifting of the freezing and thawing earth. Mason adds his own gifts as the foundation walls are poured—a wooden fish, a large marble, a 500-lira coin, a wind-up horse toy, a sparkler, woodchuck teeth and bones, tiny seashells, and a chocolate doubloon. My father-in-law Milt offers an Etruscan shard, and Em writes a note: May our minds be firm in our beliefs as this foundation, and may our thoughts pour skyward as these re-membrances go into the strong base of the chapel.

I sprinkle rugosa rose petals all around the cement top, and on the following morning, when the forms have been removed, I go out to see the foundation all set, ready to be filled with gravel, and the roses are still fresh, pink and vibrant. My friend Anne Fredericks thinks we should sprinkle the concrete with rose water. She tells me if we do, it will always retain a subtle smell of rose. Once the foundation walls are filled with gravel, she brings a basket of her luscious, pale pink garden roses over to spread about on the surface. Every phase of this building so far seems blessed, anointed with gifts and perfumed petals.

I do feel a bit like a child in the act of creation—the way I felt making a clubhouse or fort, something secret, especially mine. I think it's possible for adults to rediscover this gift of childhood—play and focus, a kind of devotion to the moment—taking that impulse and opening the aperture.

Mason in particular is having such fun with the plans. He is working and rethinking every inch of the layout, perfecting it. This morning I come to my desk and he has picked me four wild irises—they are there in the little pitcher from Assisi. He is building a model of Little Rose Chapel to scale so that we can visualize all the elements. The roof lifts off, so you can peek inside and count the floor tiles. He has even made a tiny gold wire figurine that is supposed to be me.

Starting with a plain two-by-four, Mason goes to work on the cross. We have decided on a Celtic design, which includes the feminine circle as well as the horizontal and vertical lines of the cross. Mason adds a Byzantine touch to the ends, a threefold embellishment, which is lovely, elegant. He then carves a trough in each piece of wood, giving it more depth, and paints the entire carving a rust red, which is the traditional base for gold leaf.

With a squirrel-tail brush, he begins the laborious work of gilding, but to him it is pure pleasure. He is never happier than when he can lock himself away in his room and work on some project. I would never have the patience for the itsy-bitsy handling of material as fragile as gold leaf. Sheet by delicate sheet, he places the breathy pieces of gold leaf down on the tacky surface, burnishing it until it glistens.

We go through the jewel catalogue and pick out semi-precious gems to embed in the cross, one for each birth month. With gold wire, Mason bezels the gems in place and then proceeds to carve a marble base. It is a work of art. Whenever Mason takes on a project, it always seems to turn out. I have witnessed this over and over. It certainly is true with the holy water font that he carves from a ten-dollar piece of local white marble. Chip by chip, as he hammers away at this cube, spraying marble dust all over his shop—marble dust coating his eyebrows, his sweater—the block takes shape. He rubs the marble lip until it looks like it's been smoothed by a century of hands, dipping, touching, caressing it.

We have bought two Mexican stone nichos and order a third larger one, which should arrive by mid-August. Together, Mason and I select two hand-carved posts, with twining vines and clusters of grapes worked into the wood, taking them to a local sawmill, where they are cut in half lengthwise. Setting them up on bales in the barn garage, Ayler and I work on priming and painting them, layer after layer of creamy white paint. Someday Ayler will look at these pillars and think—I'm part of the chapel too. Finally, I spray the last coat with shellac and bring them into the living room, where Mason works on gilding the raised designs, not trying for exact perfection, just embellishment.

I ask my friend Summer Brenner if her son Felix, who is on his way to Prague, could look for a statue of the Infant. Felix is game. I just hope he has his mother's good taste. He ends up finding a small porcelain statue and carries it all the way home. When Summer calls me from Berkeley, I can tell she thinks the statue is pretty weird, but she boxes it up and mails it on. I am so excited to receive the package, I can hardly wait, but on opening it—there is a moment of disappointment—it is not exactly what I had imagined.

Mason thinks the statue looks like something you'd win at the midway. Bambino di Prague is written on the base. He is dressed in grey-blue, not the red and cream I'd imagined. But when I show the statue to the painter Kate Knapp,

Golden Niche,
Root Cellar Chapel

Central Altar, Root Cellar Chapel

Scandinavian
Stavkirke

(opposite) Belgium Shrine

St. Thérèse altar, Belgium Shrine

Chapel of the
Sleeping Mary,
Greek Orthodox
Chapel

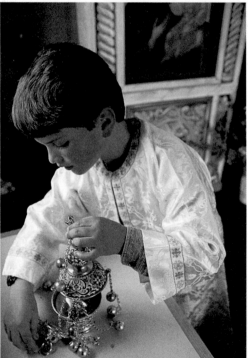

(opposite) Adirondack-
Style Chapel

(overleaf) Red Mill
Chapel in the Woods

she says that she likes the blue with the gold, and I suddenly feel myself warming up to Him.

That night I stay up until one A.M. making Him my own. Again it is that all-absorbed process of play and concentration, as if He were my own cherished doll, my infant pretend—but what is being born is something inside of me— something too mysterious to explain. I can only connect it to this feeling from childhood, where I watched the water trickle all the way from the big house down the walk to the lake front, or made an outline for a house out of raked leaves. I wrap a French lace collar around my Bambino. Now it serves as the most delicate and regal cape, and softens His ceramic clothing. Two little feathers serve as His scepters—for with gentleness He shall rule the world. I fasten the cape with a drop of hot wax, then drip wax on His face and hands, smoothing the warm, honey-scented beeswax with my fingers, gluing tiny jewels to His cross and hem and crown. I then surround Him with two white Triumphater lilies. Lighting votive candles, I contemplate His splendor, and feel a rush of heavenly love. He is now my own treasure, or I am His. It is not idolatry, the worship of an object, but something far subtler.

A big picture book, St. Thérèse and Lisieux, *arrives, and I read about how the Carmelites decorated a wax statue of the Infant and placed Him in a crib lined with swan's down. The down was taken from the dress Thérèse wore on the day she took the habit. The tunic of the Holy Infant was also cut from that dress, and His hair was made from Thérèse's own hair, saved from when she was a child. The Infant's crib is lined with a tiny rope of pearls, and He is preserved in a red casket-like enclosure—all of which seems more than a little bit creepy, but at the same time it is strangely appealing. It is the child mind at work, inventing, dressing, and preserving the holy doll through adoration and attention. I am reminded of the way I felt when I filled a shoebox with grass and made a special bed for some small dead bird, honoring and blessing its life.*

"Out of the attic of the world comes the Catholic faith," with its relics and bones, with its scraps of cloth. Is this all illusion, superstition, as my father might say, or a way of preserving something sacred that still resides in the physical world—like a hint of perfume caught in the weave of a scarf? Perhaps the sacred, which I think of as "unseen," can linger in these physical remains—and as with the effects of a homeopathic remedy, the smaller the dilution, the more potent it becomes.

I think of the childless nuns adoring their Infant, loving Him more dearly than many mothers love their own sons. I think of the softness of swan's down, and little Thérèse giving up her life of luxuries so eagerly, the quiet moment when she realized her "Little Way"—how she triumphed over her own fiery temperament. Will she help me master mine as well?

I would like to have Little Rose Chapel ready for dedication by October1st, her feast day, but I know that's impossible. Everything takes so much time. There are so many decisions. We might as well be building an entire house. Jeff Albert will not be able to begin the stone masonry until fall, and he thinks it will take him a month to do the exterior work alone.

Em and Milt want to give us a pink marble statue of Mary from the island of Torcello. The statue dates back to A.D. 700, and has broken in half, but we all know that Mason will be able to mend her. I think of the statue coming from that distant island where Venice actually began, how she must have been wrapped in layers of velvet as she sailed away in some black gondola. Did she weep, as I did when I had to leave Venice as a ten-year-old? I imagine that she will be happy again now, gracing the wall of our chapel. It was in Venice more recently that I decided to become a Catholic, and so this ancient statue has special meaning for me.

Entering San Marco, it was a bit like being draped with a dark silken veil, or anointed with some aromatic oil. I was drawn to the front of the grand basilica, where the priest was chanting in the echoing immensity. The worshippers answered. The air was cool. I felt vulnerable, yet full of wonder. Looking up at the golden curves of the ceiling covered with shining mosaics, the Byzantine shape and splendor of the place mesmerized me, and then the choir stood and began to sing and I felt some old presence sweeping through me—it made me feel this boundless joy and sadness both, as if I were finally coming home after a long, lonely journey—it was the painful feeling of great relief, warm water rushing over a frozen heart, the shock of transformation, for here in this strange place, this magnificent edifice, filled with the haunting sound of light making its way through darkness—and it sounded like the sea and waves were answering the calling shore, the tones of the Father, the deep sea tones, amidst the bells that began up above—it was simply too beautiful to bear, and it made me weep, with joy or sorrow I didn't know, as if a hand were passing up and down my spine, stroking me, pulling grief and emptiness out.

I fled the basilica, afraid that I might weep and weep until there was nothing left of me, that I would melt and slip into some minor canal and be just one more essence added to the mix. This beautiful city frightened me, as a powerful love might terrify a woman. I was not sure that I was up to it, up to being broken open, wanting it and yet turning away, running for safety, for cover.

44

But once the Holy Spirit has seized you, there is no place to hide. Step by step, I made my way until I found a church and a priest I liked. The creation of our chapel is in some ways a response to this experience in the Basilica San Marco— a simple thank-you note made out of stone and wood.

PART TWO

Holy Country, Southwest

Dear Lord, Thank You for giving me
the kind of life I would give myself.

—a child's entry
chapel notebook, Chimayó

Straw Bale Milagro Chapel Elgin, Arizona

Instead of throwing a big splashy party for her fiftieth birthday, the sculptor Patsy Lowry decided to celebrate her coming-of-age in a bronze foundry. She took fifteen hundred feet of aluminum foil and covered the entire room, asking her friends to bring candles, flowers, or shrine objects. One of her guests, Bill Brophy, suggested that she come down to the Babacomari Ranch and build a little roadside shrine—it would be his fiftieth-birthday present to her.

Bill's mother and Patsy's grandmother had been life-long friends, and so Patsy had spent a good deal of time at the ranch throughout the years. "I love the peace of the open spaces," Patsy says. "I look out across the dry arid land and feel such solitude. It has captured my heart."

Bill wanted to build the shrine out of hay bales, a currently popular method of construction, where large bales are stacked and supported by Rebar, then covered with chicken wire and sprayed with stucco. The thick-walled adobe look is very solid and fire resistant. But when Patsy saw the size of the bales—$2\frac{1}{2} \times 4$ feet—she realized that they had to create something larger than a shrine; they needed to build a chapel.

Bill agreed to the larger space, 18×22 feet, but the location of the chapel was their first dispute. "We're both such strong-willed characters. I won out, since it was my birthday present, after all. I wanted the chapel to look out over these rolling hills, to be a bit separate from the ranch house. And now I realize how important that sense of elevation was to retain the right magic and mystery."

She designed the chapel on the spot, walking it off with string. "I've never designed a building before, but I felt like I was a vehicle for this. I had a powerful sense that there was a higher purpose to this work."

Things went smoothly. The initial construction took place very quickly. As it all came together, Patsy walked up the hill and looked at her little chapel and thought—*This* is religion. "I was inspired. Everywhere I went I found

something that fit. I took a walk and saw this blue door, and said, *Oh hello, you must be my door!* It didn't take a whole lot of money. Everything just fell into place."

Patsy believes that the land is sacred, and she wanted to create something that looked like it had grown right out of the earth. The chapel does rise like the prow of a boat facing the wind of the desert. Instead of a buxom woman carved out of wood, there is a weathered cross made from a barn post and abandoned railroad ties. A statue of Mary stands beneath in a grotto of stone culled from a nearby stream. Patsy recalls how hot it was when the chapel was under construction, but how she and the foreman, Edguardo Yslava, drove the ranch truck down to the river, and handpicked every stone. The plaster statue, hand-painted with windwashed lavenders, pinks, and blues, is surrounded by shells gathered from the beaches of Mexico, as if some ancient ocean had completely dried up and left this chapel sailing.

The "angel wing walls" of the *milagro* chapel are sponge-painted with layers of pink and yellow until the undulating surface reveals itself like the colors of dawn light. Patsy points out the *bancos*, or seats, attached to the exterior—one rests beneath a stout cross-shaped window. The *bancos* are simply straw bales covered with stucco, but they make perfect benches. "I wanted to offer comfort to people. Religion is within, and holy spaces bring a person closer to that holy personal self."

The embracing walls obscure the entrance—we have to walk around. It reminds me that there is always more interest in a doorway that is not too obviously revealed. The remnant part of us that still lives back in spiritual childhood likes to be surprised, likes discovering passageways, secret cubbyholes, an unusual entrance. Entering the chapel doorway, surrounded by hand-painted flowers and icons, tendrils and angels all linked together, you feel as if you are entering a sacred garden—there is something wholly feminine here, honoring yet transforming the age-old traditions.

Patsy walks in, not in a state of hushed reverence, but very much at home, as all of Mexico is at home in her places of worship, decorating shrines with rosary beads, photos, and flowers, making the personal holy, even if it's just a little altar corner in the living room with Christmas tree lights and candles burning next to the family TV set.

"When Mexican women come to the chapel, they often weep," Patsy says, and here in this small cool space with its packed dirt floor, I can understand why. We are protected from the harsh sun, though the chapel windows are blazing with light. The ceiling is covered with the sharp barbed ribs of ocotillo, and the altar of adobe steps holds a glittering array of Mexican crosses, tin angels, a bulging red glass heart, banks of candles amongst ceramic birds and baskets of flowers. I am stunned by the excellence of excess.

Amidst all this, I pick up a piece of paper and read an offering left by a woman named Elizabeth, 3/10/96. It is addressed to Our Lady of Guadalupe, who stands beneath a shower of gargantuan roses in the right-hand corner of the room.

I offer to you my everything, my soul, the histories of my supposed heritage, the sad and lonely tales of youth, the stories from my daily life. My breast is here for your power, my age and sex but that of a little girl in your presence. Please take me in, for it is truly all I can give you in exchange for your awe. My dreams are in my open hands. I surrender. But I sacrifice all of my petty ideals and hopes for a chance to listen just briefly to your wise silence. The wind rolls over me and I am a stone. My blood rushes through me and I wait. Call me. We portray you with light, glitter and colorful glory, but you stand beyond reach of our earth, held by tethers of adornment. Do you quiver with our injustices? Or watch my self-reflective tears with reserve? I come to you for help. I come because you know. And I can only wonder. I am here if you would touch me with your starry hands. My head is bowed in respect for you. I am simple. I am humble. My worship is my love.

51

We place tall standing candles, each one a different height, around the statue of Our Lady of Guadalupe. The afternoon sun streams through the window and dances over the wild engorged roses on the corner wall. She is in her glory—illuminated, a golden coin on her dress ablaze. The chapel is alive with light.

A statue of San Ignacio, the patron saint of the ranch and chapel, stands on the second tier with rosary beads around his neck. "When I went to Spain," Patsy tells us, "I found this little shop in Madrid that makes religious sculpture out of plaster, and I asked them if they had a San Ignacio. They said no, so I asked them if they could make one for me, and they said yes, but it would take six weeks. I returned to collect him, and carried him all the way home. But I was always bothered by his baldness, you know. He looks a bit like a plucked chicken! I tried to figure out what to put on his head, and when I found this old horse shoe, which is only natural because this *is* a working cattle ranch, I put it around his head and it looks just like a halo—I love it!"

When she opens a small wooden "show me" door set into the wall, the raw hay-bale structure is displayed, with various prayer cards and emblems stuck into the surface, *milagro* medals (miracle talismans) outlining the whole. Even a silver belt buckle with a bronze horse's head seems to be perfectly placed, stuck into the straw. Names of family members are written in script on the frame of the door, and a photograph of the matriarch is displayed, along with an heirloom silver spoon.

Rising from the rough rocks strewn in the corner of the floor, a painted silver cross outlined in gold sprouts unexpectedly. Patsy is reminded of how Edguardo kicked over the paint pot and it splashed against the wall. She responded by getting out the gold paint bucket, quickly redeeming the mistake.

"Art springs from the everyday and delves into the mysterious and mystical. The artist opens inner doors and presents them to the world. I've been trying my whole life to do something of significance, with meaning and beauty, and this is it. It's hard to have it so far away."

While Lowry was building and decorating the chapel back in 1992, she had to make numerous trips south, driving back and forth between her home in Paradise Valley and the ranch in Santa Cruz County, the southernmost region of the state. "It was a passion, an obsession," she explains.

The dedication of the chapel, on the Feast of the Immaculate Conception, December 8th, 1992, was another kind of birth. It was a stormy, rainy day, and the priest who came to bless the chapel, Father Greg, arrived from

Sierra Vista wearing Father Kino's ceremonial stole from the 1800s. In the service he said, "While the hearth has always been considered the heart of the home, so the *capilla* is the heart of the *rancho*. It was the *capilla* that was set on the highest point of land, and it was the *capilla* that blessed the fields and the animals by its mere presence, a reminder that all goodness comes from a loving and merciful God." Father Greg proceeded to read from Scripture, and then as he blessed the entrance, blessed the image of San Ignacio as well as the altar, drops of holy water streamed down the face of a silver angel embedded in the wall.

Since the day of the dedication, there have been marriages celebrated and losses mourned. The Yslavas' daughter rode sidesaddle up to the chapel for her wedding ceremony, and Patsy presided over the blessing of two grandchildren of her best friend. "We had four generations of women all gathered together, and it was powerful. I felt honored." Turning up the portable radio they played *Love Makes the World Go Round,* and danced a celebratory dance.

One feels the pulse beat of life here in this small chapel with its glittering surfaces. One small glass mosaic cross was made from a broken TV screen, another friendly accident. "It felt natural to include the pieces and make something beautiful out of them," she says. In a similar way, one senses an acceptance of death here. Perhaps it is partly due to the Latin influence, where life and death are intimately linked. The Day of the Dead is not about spooks and skeletons. It is about the intimate connection the living have with those who have passed. *"Come Dear Spirits, and warm your hands over the candle flames."* Here in the *capilla,* beloved family members are remembered. Pictures of three Brophy children rest on the steps of the altar, with a loving tribute written by a father.

Bill Brophy also died in 1994. Patsy acknowledges that it was a time of letting go. "Death is about releasing one's hold, and when Bill died, it was a major trauma in my life, because I not only lost my dear friend, but I lost my place at the ranch too. I can go back and visit, but it's not the same. Now the chapel belongs to the world. When I was working on it, I wanted every part of the chapel to be a work of art. Now others come and leave offerings, adding to the spirit of the place. It took me nine months to create this chapel, and as with any child, you have a unique, intimate connection. I don't believe that will ever change.

"As my daughter told Bill before he died—she went into the ranch house and said to him, 'Bill, thank you for letting my mother put herself on your hill. I've seen pictures, but they didn't prepare me for what I experienced. Walking inside that chapel was like walking into my mother's heart and soul.'"

LORETO MENDEZ AND EARL NIICHEL

Rosicrucian Temple Mowry, Arizona

There have been a few changes made since I was last here. Lori has painted columns on either side of the vibrant blue doors and placed a hollowed-out swan with a red rose just within the entrance to use as a holy water font, but the mysterious mood and scent of roses inside the temple is the same. I realize, in part, that this hush of feeling comes from the fact that there are no windows, only the two heavy doors, partially closed now. A crack of light illuminates a crystal angel set at the foot of the Virgin Mary, making a dazzle in the back corner, while a skylight above the triangular altar gives this dark temple a glimpse of heaven. Earl says that the light from the sky portal changes at various times of day, moving across the wall, and that the architecture of the temple relates to Egyptology.

"The triangular altar," Lori explains, "represents the *Shekinah,* or the feminine aspect of God. The energy around that is very creative." On the altar stands a Hermetic cross—with symbols from the kabala that point to the twenty-two paths to God. The Rosicrucians do not adhere to any religious tenets, but their teachings are devoted to seeking individual, inner wisdom while offering an experience of inner peace.

Here in Lori and Earl's intimate temple space, I see that the Infant of Prague has been moved to the high altar. I ask Lori what He means to her, and she tells me that after her father's death, the Infant of Prague appeared to her as she was coming out of a very deep sleep. "I wasn't aware of who He was at the time, so I began to learn about the original statue," which had originally

55

been a wedding present to a Spanish Princess. At the end of her life, she gave the statue to a monastery, which was subsequently ransacked, the holy statue discarded in the rubble. The monks had to flee, but Father Cyrillus had recurring dreams about the Infant. He begged his abbot to let him go back to Prague in search of the statue. When he found Him, the hands were broken off, but he heard this message distinctly—*Fix My Hands and I Will Bless You*. After the holy hands were mended, many miracles began to occur. To this day they still continue.

Lori has her own personal story about finding her statue. She was in the Salvation Army one day, when she happened to spot an Infant of Prague on the counter. "Of course I went right to Him, but was informed by the clerk that He had already been taken by another lady who was putting things aside. So, I walked away, but after a while the clerk came up to me and asked if I still wanted the statue. She told me that it had been put back. The lady who had almost bought Him decided against it because His hands were broken. You can imagine my reaction! My whole system seemed to hum—it was as if I could hardly believe my ears. All I could do was say that I would fix them." After that the Infant became her own special guardian. She believes the statue represents the close connection to the Divine Child that resides within each one of us.

A few chairs are placed in the back of the temple, and I imagine that Lori and Earl come here often to meditate or pray on the essence of the opening rose, an image central to the Rosicrucian philosophy. Having their own sacred space doesn't prevent them from finding religious community in Tucson, an hour away, where they attended the Church of the Cosmic Christ, a metaphysical church with an Italian kabalistic minister.

Lori is a Mexican American, raised a traditional Catholic, but now she's devoted to the study of ancient mystical doctrines, learning how they apply to modern-day life. The goal of Rosicrucian philosophy is to give everyone the means to live in cosmic harmony on physical, mental, emotional, and spiritual planes and to attain a state of profound peace. There are various indications of how to ascend to the spiritual sanctum—the highest plane of consciousness—through purification, visualization, and meditation. "You can learn from everybody," Lori says in her open, enthusiastic manner. "You have to keep your mind open—soul experiences can come from some very unusual places!"

The elements of earth and water seem to combine within each handmade tile, for they have used both blue and pinkish colors. "The masons sprinkled powdered dye into the cement and then swirled the colors around with a pencil. They'd hang onto this huge bar and press it down and when it came up, you'd have one tile. They made six hundred of them, and only charged fifty cents apiece."

These same tiles extend outside as well, and cover a small patio area to the side of the temple. Here Lori's grandchildren have placed their own small, hand-painted tiles into the adobe wall. How nice, I think, to include the children in this family edifice. The boys' representations of God are powerful, a bit ominous— while the girls have painted pretty pictures of flowers and a shining sun. "But this one fascinated me," Lori says. "It was this dark thing with a white light, and I asked Philip—*What* is *that?* 'Well, that's the tunnel you go through when you die,' he said. John's was a tornado, and I said—How is *that* going to fit in here? And he said 'Because it shows you the power of God.' Then I felt really *dumb*," Lori laughs. She laughs so easily, and finds humor in almost everything. "One of the girls did a cross, and made a hole in it, and I thought—Hey, I could use that as a light switch!"

As we walk back to the house, Lori tells me that she had a very difficult twenty-eight-year marriage with a man who was verbally abusive. "But he was the father of my five children, so I tried and tried to make it work. Of course, I didn't believe in divorce, but finally I realized I couldn't make it any better, and had to do something for myself."

She then enjoyed a very happy, though brief, second marriage, cut short by illness. "He retired in May and was gone by September," she recalls. Bereft, she worked on the construction of their octagonal log home by herself for four lonely years. "But God was good to me. He led Earl here all the way from Iowa."

Earl had been on his own pilgrimage, camping out with his horse and dog for over a year, slowly moving from ranch to ranch all over southern Arizona, recording his journey in a big notebook, until one day he rode into Patagonia, and someone suggested that he visit Lori's place out in Mowry. "When I arrived, Lori wasn't here," he admits, "but I peeked in the window and just fell in love with everything I saw. There was a guitar leaning against the davenport, a piano and an old saddle. *So,* I thought—the lady plays the guitar and piano, and rides a horse. But she doesn't do any of the above!"

"They're all props," she laughs. "False advertising."

The two of them spent an entire year celebrating their honeymoon by taking a trip in each of the four directions, but it was only afterwards that she confessed her dream of wanting to have her own chapel. "I wanted a place where I could feel safe, a sanctuary from the outside world. My dream was to have one where you'd go underground—I wanted to build it out of rock, and then you'd find this beautiful crystal and you'd sit on top of it. I know that sounds far out, a fantasy. But when I told Earl about wanting a chapel, he said—'Well, let's do it.' He had fallen in love with adobe, so we made it out of adobe bricks."

Before the temple was completed, their friends Carl and Chris wanted to have a wedding ceremony there. The walls and roof were up, but nothing was plastered and there was no floor. "It was very crude. I would have been happy with a dirt floor, but this Iowan man!" she laughs.

"I had eight grandchildren here at the house at the time, and we wanted them to sing *Here Comes the Bride, All Dressed in White,* but then I thought— Hmm, what's the rest of it? So I told them, just hum the tune. We called them— The Whispering Rose Hummers. So all the grandchildren came, but they didn't understand the service—it wasn't a Catholic Mass, the bride wasn't dressed up in a white gown, and then Carl and Chris had sage incense—they wanted to cleanse the air and the whole nine yards. So we took it to the grandkids and they went—*Oh my Grande, what are we going to do with her? She does such weird things!* But by the end, they realized there was a sacredness to this."

Though this small family temple is only 14 × 18 feet, they managed to squeeze fifty people inside for Lori's daughter's wedding. "There were another hundred standing outside," Earl adds. "We had just about every color and creed all gathered together, people from across the border, people from every- where—it was quite a celebration."

At first they were worried about how the local priest would react to their non-traditional temple, but luckily they found Reverend Jenkins from the Community Church in Patagonia, who was quite open-minded. When he saw the statue of the Buddha on the floor, he began to chant, *"Ommm."* They both smile recalling the incident.

Since my past visit, Lori also presided over the wedding of Margie and Charlie, my hosts at the nearby Poco Toro Ranch. "It was so profound we all

wept, especially the groom! It made us feel very humble and honored to be witnesses."

Margie wrote the following prayer, which she read during the ceremony:

Oh God, Our Father in Heaven
We stand before You very happy
But somewhat nervous

We feel You brought us together in the beginning
Because we feel we were surely meant for each other

You knew this and You helped our Love grow
And are at this moment with us in a special way

59

In this very special place
Built in Your honor, with total Love and Sincerity

We ask that You stay by our side in the days ahead
Protect us from anything, which might harm this union
Give us courage when burdens come our way
Teach us to forgive one another when we fail
Teach us patience and understanding

Help us always to remember we love each other dearly
We give thanks to You for bringing us together
Please bless us Oh Lord
And what we are doing Amen

Tomorrow Lori will be marrying a couple out in the San Rafael Valley. She has become an ordained minister. I ask her what she will wear, and she points to a painting over their fireplace. There is a Mayan princess, standing before a sunset, with the star of Venus shining in the evening sky. She is wearing a white robe with colorful braid running around the edges. "I just fell in love with that painting and had to have it. It brings together all time for me."

"But what's odd," Earl adds, "is that someone gave Lori the exact same robe." She goes into the bedroom and gets it, and yes, it is identical. She will wear the ceremonial robe at the wedding tomorrow. "This young couple built their own altar out of rocks. They wanted their service to be out in the open."

Earl goes on to say, "I don't think either one of us really knew why we built our chapel. It just seemed like something we should do."

"It was like a dream," Lori adds.

"It's taken on vibrations, tremendously different than when it was first built—then it was just a building. Now, it feels like a very powerful place."

Essene Temple Patagonia, Arizona

It's not surprising that Gabriel Cousens chose Patagonia, one of the most magical and healing places I know, as the home for his Essene Temple. This small cylindrical temple with its pyramid-shaped roof, based on the dimensions of the Great Pyramid, stands at the foot of Red Mountain on the outskirts of town. Gabriel, a medical doctor, runs the *Tree of Life Rejuvenation Center* here, a rather low-key place, still under construction, but despite the somewhat transient feel, it is apparent that the staff members live a good life, raising their own food and maintaining a rather rigorous spiritual practice.

As we talk, Gabriel and I soon discover that we shared a similar Midwestern, athletically oriented, suburban background. During his high school years in Highland Park, he was known for his skill as a quarterback. In fact his athletic practice kept him from being bar mitzvahed at the traditional age. Though it may seem a leap—from physical prowess to spiritual fitness—a certain strength of ego and focus of direction have served him well in both fields.

Graduating from Amherst College, he and his wife moved to New York City, where he attended Columbia Medical School—"A process not designed for human beings," he says. "I was trained as a psychiatrist first, and then went on to learn about homeopathy." After medical school, Gabriel and his wife lived in Harlem for several years, where they were involved with a community-controlled school, about a block from Harlem Hospital. "We set up a clinic in the school, and within a week we examined five hundred kids and found all kinds of problems. We got some funding and trained mothers in the community, so that they could become health aides. The help was available, people just didn't know how to get it."

The Cousens then moved on to California, where they were active in anti-war protests, but finally Gabriel realized that his outwardly active life was not inwardly very peaceful. "What concerned me even more was that our

tactics were not much different than those of the opposition." It was at this point that he dropped his political activities and began what turned out to be a cycle of meditation, prayer, and fasting, traveling to India to be with Muktananda for the last years of his life. Gabriel was one of the few non-swamis who received Muktananda's blessing to awaken kundalini energy through direct touch. "I would meditate for six hours a day, and chant a lot and sit quietly with him for hours, and a lot of things happened. When I came back, I was looking for a metaphor that would be closer to what I was trying to teach in the West, and I gravitated to the Essene tradition, what I would call shamanic Judaism."

Though his concerns are planetary and cosmic, he is also used to dealing with one patient at a time. One has to begin with the individual. He is a great believer in what could almost be called the "homespun remedies" of good air, pure water and diet, sunlight, rest, and adequate exercise. It does seem obvious that when we eat in a healthy, harmonious way, our ability to commune with the Divine is enhanced.

Gabriel says that he usually recommends two week-long fasts a year. "During that fast we are doing yoga, meditating twice a day, walking, teaching breathing exercises, and getting people inspired—it's a total experience." A lot of addictive behavior, Gabriel believes, has to do with neuro-transmitter imbalances—"You keep taking drugs to stimulate pleasure centers, and there are much healthier ways to do that." They are finding that people need different diets depending on whether they are fast or slow oxidizers. Finding peace with the body seems to be the starting point, though Gabriel's medical training as a psychiatrist also helps him counsel individuals and couples.

Gabriel speaks to us about his belief that people everywhere are gaining similar insights—that we can no longer remain isolated, religious separat-ists—that we have to acknowledge on some higher level that we are One, de-spite our individual beliefs and practices. This is something I have always in-nately believed. Even as a teenager, stopping at the Baha'i Temple north of Chicago, I felt moved by their teachings, which emphasize the spiritual unity of all mankind. Gabriel would expand on that to say "the unity of all living things."

After lunch, we walk up the path to take part in the Friday evening meditation service that begins in a sacred circle just outside the temple. This meadow in the foothills is so beautiful to me, I already feel as if I've entered a mildly euphoric state. I join the group and sit before the fire as the sun sets behind the Patagonia Mountains. Again, this feeling that I am at home, at peace within myself here.

Together, we enter the temple for the Shabbat ser-vice. It is a warm and comforting space with its undu lating pink walls barely lit. The desert at this altitude gets cool at night, but solar panels give enough energy to pump warm water through coils embedded in the tachyonized rammed-earth floor. At the center of the room is a sunken pit containing a ninety-pound trans-mitter crystal. A solar light placed beneath it represents the eternal light of the soul that is always burning. As the room gets darker, the crystal glows within a Star of David that is laid in shining copper on the floor.

Everyone chooses a place on a cushion around the perimeter of the room. There are few aesthetic decora-tions to distract one here. The meditation continues for about ten minutes before a hand-cleansing ritual begins. Simply and mindfully, a bowl of water is passed from hand to hand, each person holding it for the next. Then we each take turns drying that person's hands—a gesture of serving the other, connecting, before we share a loaf of Essene bread, passing it also from hand to hand, feeding each other. I am hungry, and this slightly sweet, sun-baked bread is both filling and delicious.

Gabriel says, "We meditate, not to attain God, but to become aware of the God within us." There is something about the tone of this evening ritual that is very profound—it enters me deeply and stays there, humming.

The next morning I return for morning sunrise meditation, which honors the planet, our Mother Earth. It is cold, and I am offered a heavy woolen blanket to drape over my shoulders and legs. Gabriel sits beneath the tent-like covering of his traditional prayer shawl. As the sun breaks over the eastern rim, and the morning frost melts into dew, I am conscious that we are now facing the opposite direction from the night before. Though this may seem obvious, it is interesting to actually experience the physical shift.

After morning meditation, Gabriel, Donna, and I retreat to the temple and talk more about the ancient Essenes. Some claim that Jesus, Joseph, and Mary were all part of this early mystical sect of Judaism. From what I gather, these early Jews led very pure lives, eating simply, studying and praying deeply, and following a mystical path. "They began to form communities about 186 B.C.," Gabriel explains, "and were called the Pious Ones, very involved with a right relationship with Nature. A lot of what they did can serve as a model that could help us heal and transform the world today."

The Romans made quite an effort to wipe out the Essenes and all their literature. They punished anyone who was a vegetarian. It was a crime. "Today some contemporary Essenes focus on Jesus," Gabriel explains, "because he was the most famous member of their sect, while others focus on the Essene Way of Life, which is what he taught. It's a meeting place for Christians and Jews."

Even though the temple is a mystical Jewish temple, it's used in such a way that it honors everyone. "It is not a single-focus community. No one says—You can only do it this way. We have people here who are Christian, Jewish, Zen, Hindu, whatever. Visitors and patients have come here from over twenty-four different nations."

More often than not, I am finding a similar ecumenical approach with those involved with private chapels—they seem to be a lot more tolerant and open, and a lot less arrogant—*My way is the only way.* Perhaps this desire to come together, honoring differences and recognizing our common belief in a Higher Power, forecasts a tendency that organized religions will begin to emulate.

Gabriel says that he tries to follow the traditional Jewish traditions and is learning to read the Torah. "I'm kind of a late connector," he admits. "I was raised in Reform Judaism, where it was more casual. I wasn't bar mitzvahed till I was forty-four."

Several old Tibetan bowls are displayed on the floor before his meditation pad—he normally plays them during group meditation. But now he rings the rim and the resonance seems to go on and on—he opens his mouth to receive the tone and almost drinks it in, warping the vibration to make little undulations of sound. As he plays, one tone vibrates over another, a deep underwater gong beneath a high, almost piercing vibration.

"A lot of the work I'm doing," Gabriel says, "is trying to get people back to a more earth based experience of things. Using kabalistic terminology, you'd say—the *Shekinah* energy—reestablishing the feminine, and that is not just female, but it is considered the spirit in all things, the feminine aspect of God, bringing that back. The Hebrew tradition is totally earth based. It's based on the moon cycle, and even though it's been dominated by more left-brain thinking, its prophetic roots are really in the feminine."

VALER AND JOSIAH AUSTIN

Pearce, Arizona,
and Beyond

El Coronado Ranch Chapel

Driving south from Dragoon through a verdant agricultural valley where walnuts and pistachios grow, the road is long and straight, and there are not many restaurants, until we hit upon a little Mexican cafe, and have some mouthwatering chicken enchiladas with sour cream and green chile sauce. I ask the friendly Mexican American waitress if she knows of any private chapels, and her eyes light up—she has heard about Valer's stone chapel up in the foothills of the Chiricahuas, but she wants to tell me a story about a local boy who was riding his bicycle and got hit by a car, how he never should have survived the accident, but how an old man appeared out of nowhere and prayed over him and the boy pulled through. There is religion in this woman's eyes, as if she has marked this holy spot in her mind. I feel the presence of the Lord alive in her, and am amazed to keep meeting person after person who seems to have this inner light.

We head on, following Valer's precise directions. The foothills have a dry and dusty quality, but soon oak and cottonwood appear. Turning in at the EC ranch gate, we see a plaque that describes the Austins as "Environmentalists of the Year." We pull up before a sprawling white adobe home, with a large gracious oak out front. The house, purchased years ago from the University of Arizona, is magnificent—water and greenery everywhere. I've never seen such lushness in this desert climate. A natural stream that comes out of the high rocky Chiricahuas is diverted through small rock-lined gullies that flow even faster because of their narrowness—the gravitational pull moves the water along as it spills into burbling fountains before continuing downhill. Two large ponds stand between the house and chapel, which I can see through the trees— what an incredible setting. The place is so beautiful, grand, and restful. Two big dogs come running out to greet us, with a toddling Mexican baby following. I hear someone call, *"Chica,"* and then there is Valer in her hiking boots and blue jeans, warm and welcoming.

We are eager to get some shots of the chapel in the afternoon light. It looks like the sun will disappear behind the mountains by four o'clock. So Donna sets up, and Valer and I talk as if we were old friends. I find it easy to ask her personal questions, how she came to Catholicism in the first place.

She begins by saying that she lived in Paris for a year as a teenager. "I went there supposedly for my year abroad to learn language and to study, but instead I was interested in religion." She goes on to describe an unusual, almost visionary experience she had during that time. Taken on a tour of St. Peter's Basilica in Rome, Valer left her group and sat in a pew and just stared at the stone floor for almost an hour. "Clearly I was not aware of the church or anything—I was just aware of this huge light, and I was gone in that light for quite a period of time. Afterwards I felt very peaceful, but I just took it in stride. As a teenager you are in so much turmoil, but this was a visitation of peacefulness."

Valer feels that there is not only a lot of prejudice against Catholics in America today, but also against anyone who follows a spiritual path. While many of the original small, private chapels in Europe were built because of persecution, here in the "land of the free" prejudice is a more subtle thing, and perhaps even more insidious as it often takes the form of an undermining mockery or intellectual cynicism. Perhaps we are not as tolerant as we pretend. Perhaps we only give lip service to religious freedom. Valer and I agree how important it is not to judge each other's beliefs—how we are all basically one. No matter where we live or what we practice, our spiritual needs are as various and similar as our other basic human needs. Wouldn't it be strange if everyone on Earth dressed alike, ate the exact same food, and lived in similar houses?

Valer goes on to describe another experience she had as a teenager when she was considering conversion. Sister Jean-Marie, a nun who had taken an interest in her, took Valer to a Carmelite wedding—the marriage of an initiate to Christ. The father of the bride actually walked this young girl, Valer's age, down the aisle. She was dressed in a beautiful bridal gown, but when she went behind the grill, her dress was taken and her hair was shaved off. She was then clothed entirely in black. Now she was dead to the world. They laid the girl on the floor in the form of the crucifix, and began chanting over her.

St. Thérèse, also a Carmelite, underwent a similar ceremony, but I wonder if such rituals are still performed today in this age of anonymous nuns who walk the streets dressed like the rest of us. There is something powerful and strong and eerie about the intensity of this spiritual marriage Valer witnessed. It seems akin to the extreme practices of the *Penitentes*. But even those traditions may have been tempered for modern times, as if true believers today could not take such strenuous worship. People often smirk when they speak of women crawling on their knees to the doors of a cathedral, as if such profound humility were degrading or ridiculous.

"When we moved out here, my conversion seemed to have made good sense, because so much of this world is Catholic." A good portion of the Austins' ranch reaches into Mexico, and some of the men who work here came north to help build the chapel. "These men are very good stonemasons. It's an art that they have that is so superior. They are actually Indians, and they have this ability almost built in—when you think of the Aztecs, it was rock they used as their medium."

We walk down to the chapel, and sit on the long wooden bench that rests before the picture window. The glass looks out at the mountains and a rushing stream. "Taz," short for Tasmanian Devil, her big black dog, follows us inside, but Valer says, "Out," when he comes into the chapel—no devil dogs allowed.

"I did feel that this ranch is so remote, and we are visited by lots of people—they come here to relax and to think and it's generally at a time of celebration, Christmas or Easter or Thanksgiving, and we often have a service and it seemed nice to have a place where that service could be held."

At New Year's a group of family and friends stood in a circle and everyone put different thoughts or poems into a hat, and then each person took out a slip of paper and read. If anyone had something to say, they spoke, and if they didn't, that was all right too. At Christmastime the family lays out a beautiful hand-carved Austrian crèche on the altar. Then they light a candle and sing.

I am impressed by the artistry of the masonry, a smooth wall of rock on the outside as well as a flat wall of rock on the inside. In between these surfaces lie cement and rocks, like a sandwich. The stone structure was built with very simple tools, a crowbar, chisel, some hammers, and a level. But when they started the stone work, Valer saw that it was going to be a bit too dark. "I thought, it's going to need some lightness. The men knew I liked to paint, so they said, 'Why not *pinturas*?' I thought about traditional paintings in chapels, how they were all done with fresco, but I didn't know anything about fresco. It was much more complicated than I realized. I went to an extended workshop outside of Rome, where I worked on a trial panel, then I came back to the States and was an apprentice to Ben Long. Basically what I did was grind his paint and mix his colors. You make the powder for the paints very fine, because the pigments are diluted in water, and then they are sucked into the wall, almost like a tattoo effect."

Valer goes on to describe the process. "On the next to last layer of plaster the artist does a drawing with earth red paint, called a *scenopia*. At that point, in Italy, they would invite in the patron, and they'd all look at the design on the wall, and then the patron might say, 'Take my cousin out and put my girlfriend in.' Any change would be made at that point.

"On top of the *scenopia,* you would lay your final layer of plaster, which is a very thin layer, containing more lime than the others. Your cartoon is transferred to this last outer layer by incising, or a process called pouncing—little pin pricks mark the lines of the figure or forms of the painting, and then you take some charcoal and you *pounce.* Sometimes you can still see little charcoal lines in old frescoes.

"On the morning when you apply your plaster for that day, you have to be patient, for it can't be too wet or the paint picks up the plaster underneath and the color turns to mud. You have to feel it. If it starts to draw in the pigment, then it's ready. You can't just put any color on top of any other color—it's almost like glazing."

Valer explains how the artist has to try and make her *journata,* or day's work, end where the division doesn't matter, because one can not get the exact same color from day to day. She points out the eight different divisions where she made her breaks. I am disappointed that she wasn't able to wrap it up in seven, especially since her fresco pictures the Creation story from Genesis. Beneath the painted scene that runs around the upper portion of the room the words flow together: *In the beginning the earth was without form and void Darkness was upon the face of the deep God said let there be light and he divided the light from the darkness . . .*

"I wanted the sense of forces—of gases, movement, just pure energy," Valer explains—"that was the feeling in the void. And then I wanted combustion to come out of that—Light, just bursting out. And then the gases and light formed into liquids. This part is all abstract—that isn't a sea you would swim in, and that sky isn't a sky you'd recognize. The earth is just coming into being, and then all of a sudden the moonlight is shining down, and the seasons are there and night and day—you could swim in that sea—it's full of life.

"Rather than have any intricate detail, I thought that wasn't in keeping with the sweep of it—I put the details within the text—a little trilobite, a fetus, a crustacean, then a worm and butterfly." A small turtle is included, because the Austins have a Sonoran Mud Turtle Project on the ranch, as well as a Leopard Frog and Bull Nose Snake Project. All of these creatures are incorporated into the linear part of her fresco, but she has also included other touches from the ranch and the surrounding desert—an agave, a rock that is reminiscent of Dragoon, a cowboy with an EC buckle on his belt, a mountain lion and a bear. In fact a local bear has been going on a rampage through the ranch, destroying their apple and apricot trees, tearing down limbs and wantonly feasting.

"The large Olmec head represents man's focus on the Divine," Valer explains, "and also his creative artistic talents. The Olmecs and the Mayans both worked with stone. The Indians who worked on this chapel come out of a similar tradition, so it seemed an appropriate figure."

There is a modern scene depicting the family—man, woman, and child—and then for the transition between life and death, there is a figure on a stretcher. Next there are the spirits, released from their bodies. "In a way at this point, they have lost their color—they are floating along in the spirit, and now they are becoming part of the air. Like a spiral, which goes round and turns back on itself, they also go up and become more realized—the transition is but a moment."

The altar, interestingly enough, is made out of fossilized stone that Josiah found, little fish swimming through the eons. The figure of Mary, who stands on the altar top, *The Virgin of the Smile,* is a seventeenth-century figure from Spain, her face and hands carved out of ivory.

In Barcelona, when Franco plundered the cathedral, this statue was rescued, and she became the property of Virginia Ullman, an old friend of Valer's, who came down from her home in Phoenix to visit the ranch and to celebrate her 90-something birthday. She fell in love with Valer's chapel, and gave the Austins this priceless statue. The Virgin seems to be very much at home amidst all this color, her tin star halo curving above her head, her face beatific, the gesture of her hands extremely gentle. Valer opens the brocade cloak to show us the intense turquoise of the inner robe, which has now faded to a subtle grey-blue.

> Dear dear Virginia,
>
> As I write you the rain is pouring down like a blessing on the desert, as if the whole mountain range waits to celebrate your visit here. Tomorrow everything will have grown a little higher. With you growth is possible as you make things happen. You bring people together. You are a catalyst for ecologists, artists, creative people in many fields. I am enormously touched by your gift to the chapel, for the gift of love becomes eternal.
>
> Valer

It is time for the dogs' daily walk, and Valer invites me to come along. I'm game, though I'm only wearing sandals, and ask if I shouldn't change shoes. She doesn't think that's necessary, but once we're up on the trail, climbing over rock, I'm sorry I'm not wearing the equivalent of Valer's sturdy hiking boots. Valer is small and lithe and fit. It's hard to keep up with her. But as her husband tells me later, there are not many who can.

As we climb up the canyon, she points out small stone retaining walls, called *gambions.* The same men who created the chapel put in thousands of these stone walls that catch the often violent run-off rainwater. Silt is held in place and grass seed takes root. This entire canyon is being transformed from a rocky wasteland into a lush mountain hillside. I'm beginning to understand the implications of that environmental plaque by the entrance.

The next day after a horseback ride around the ranch, Donna and I take off for New Mexico. I'm sad to leave the Austins so soon, but we have a full agenda. Deciding to be adventurous, we take a dirt road over the Chiricahuas, and by the time we descend into the small town of Animus, the sunset light is quickly becoming dusk and the huge protruding shapes of the receding mountains can be seen looming against the starry sky.

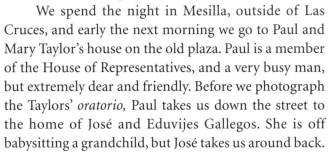

We spend the night in Mesilla, outside of Las Cruces, and early the next morning we go to Paul and Mary Taylor's house on the old plaza. Paul is a member of the House of Representatives, and a very busy man, but extremely dear and friendly. Before we photograph the Taylors' *oratorio,* Paul takes us down the street to the home of José and Eduvijes Gallegos. She is off babysitting a grandchild, but José takes us around back.

Their little family chapel looks like a run-down shed from the outside, with plastic stretched over the windows, but when José opens the door and clicks on the light, we are astounded. Paul affirms that the large statue of *Jesús el Nazareño,* central to the little peach-colored altar, is an extremely rare and unusual piece. The walls are painted lavender, and the effect is luscious. The chapel has become a bit of a storage space, with a child's purple bicycle and large sacks of chiles and potatoes in the back. Tall sticks with jingle-bell balls stand in the corner—these are used in Christmas pageants. The four rifles propped against the wall are used on Good Friday to guard the four corners of the church.

José points out a funereal-looking tableau of Jesus on the cross with various tools of torture, all made out of metal, like the little *milagros* that are sewn onto a wall hanging next to the altar. A small plastic baby is sewn there too. José claims that the *bulto* of *Jesús el Nazareño* was passed down through his wife's family for generations and that it made *muchos milagros,* many miracles, when it was taken around the fields before planting.

When we return to Paul's house in the afternoon, he allows us free rein, as the phone continues to ring for him. We wander through the maze of rooms, the house a living folk museum with priceless carvings everywhere. I am entranced by the jumble of treasures, the bounty of their lives spilling from room to room. He shows us an early New Mexican *bulto* of Santiago, and tells us a story about how he acquired it.

"Years ago, we used to have a teacher's convention in Albuquerque, and I always went to the Catholic Center because they had some of these wonderful old pieces. This fabulous New Mexican piece was ninety dollars, and I went back year after year to look at it—I just admired it so, and I guess I had been there three or four years in a row, when finally this woman said to me, 'You know if you want that, you better take it, because we're raising all our prices.' And I said, 'You know I'm a teacher, I can't afford that—I'm putting shoes on children.' And she said, 'Well, just pay something down. Do you have five dollars?' And I said yes, I have five dollars. So she said, 'Well, pay five dollars down, and then pay five dollars a month until you get it paid.' Five dollars! 'That's nothing,' I said, 'You've got to take care of your stock.' And she said, 'No, I can tell you really want it.' So, I gave her my five dollars, and she gave me a receipt and I started out the door, but she called after me, 'Aren't you going to take Santiago?' And I said, 'I can't take Santiago! You don't even *know* me. You only have five dollars, and I should take Santiago home?' She said, 'Listen, you have been here so many times, year after year.' She insisted that I take it. So she wrapped it up. Five dollars a month until the ninety dollars was paid, and so here's my Santiago. And this wonderful woman who trusted me, otherwise I'd never have him."

The statue is indeed special, delicately carved. But my favorite is a very endearing carving of "Jesus in the Temple." There is something about Him that fills me with awe, as if this carved statue actually emanates special powers. I feel taken by Him, the way you are instantly attracted to a certain new friend.

Paul tells us that there is a nice little store down on the corner of the plaza that sells *Nacimientos*. I respond by saying that I already own a crèche. "A single crèche?" he declares. "We have fifty of them!"

We tour the plaza, and down one side street I find a wonderful unpainted Saint Francis. He is missing a hand, but that doesn't bother me, for I know

Mason will be able to fix him. He is contemporary and comes from Mexico, and is not one of the more valuable, older New Mexican pieces, but there is something about his face that speaks to me.

Late that night, checking into the old-fashioned El Rey Inn in Santa Fe, which looks like it could be a stage set for a Southwestern version of a late-forties movie, I unpack the wooden Saint Francis statue and balance a mother-of-pearl dove on his one good hand. Hallmark might have sentimentalized St. Francis' relationship to animals—the Hispanic culture pictures him holding a cross and skull, contemplating death—but this revered saint did have a special connection to the world of creatures, and the animal kingdom does make us more aware of the fragile heartbeat of life, its ephemeral transience. In any case, he seems right at home here in this quiet little nest in Santa Fe, which I suddenly realize means Holy Faith.

Face of an Angel,
Martinez Chapel

(opposite) Martinez Chapel

Altar, Straw Bale Milagro Chapel
(overleaf) Straw Bale Milagro Chapel

San Ignacio, Straw Bale Milagro Chapel

(opposite) Doors and Fresco, El Coronado Ranch Chapel

(overleaf) Altar, Rosicrucian Temple

Santa Fe Santero New Mexico

Faith and spirituality permeate the culture as well as the geography here in northern New Mexico. The Sangre de Cristo (Blood of Christ) Mountains are dusted with snow as we set off for the day. Following our map, we arrive at a wonderful old stone chapel, built by Ramon Lopez's grandfather in the 1930s. Lorenzo Lopez was also a saint carver, or *santero,* and though he died two years before Ramon was born, he has always been an inspiration to his grandson.

The angular walkway with its stick fence seems a natural extension of the structure, set sturdily into the rocky hillside. We enter the cavern-like interior through a crude wooden turnstile topped by a cross. A stunted cedar has forced its way inside. Looking back out, one can see the perfectly rounded forms of Sun and Moon Mountains, once sacred to local Indians.

This is the *Capilla de San Isidro,* patron saint of farmers. To the left, on a raised bed within the chapel, a field in miniature stands, enclosed by a tiny retaining wall. Here the elder Lopez used to re-enact the story of San Isidro with wooden characters he'd made by hand, set amongst the make-believe crops. Unfortunately, the carvings that used to grace this place have all been stolen. When Ramon was in high school, he overheard some guys saying how they'd swiped the dolls and tried to sell them. Theft of sacred *bultos* is a serious problem all over the Southwest, the reason why so many of these beautiful, intimate chapels are locked up tight with massive padlocks.

Now there are only candles, set back into the rock, a perfect place for a crèche scene. They do have a Christmas celebration here, with *luminarias*—paper bags holding sand and votive candles—lining the walkway. What a won-

derful place to gather and sing. The ancient, unadorned space easily takes one back to the original holy grotto in Jerusalem.

There seems to be a deep spirituality amongst the Hispanic American people we meet. They have a gift for living into the Passion, as if their faith not only enters their thoughts and emotions, but takes hold of their bodies as well. One young girl's journal entry conveys this simply: *Dear God please take care of all of my family. I know that I should love you with all my hart, with sole, mind and musules. Aman. Senserly, Veronica*

We continue on up the mountain to meet Ramon at his house, nestled up high, around 8,000 feet. We are still adjusting to the altitude, laboring a bit with the camera bags. He gives us a warm greeting—his blue eyes have an amused glint as he watches us huff and puff.

Ramon has just been awarded one of twelve National Heritage Fellowships given out by the NEA. Modestly he says that he received this honor as a representative of many artisans, but he is clearly one of the most talented and respected amongst his fellow *santeros*.

Since the trip, he has not been able to get back to work, he admits. He has hardly touched his stack of mail. While he used to work sixteen hours a day, now he only puts in about twelve, carving *bultos* (statues of saints), *retablos* (flat paintings of saints on wood), and *reredos* (altar screens). He also paints on stretched buffalo hide, carves furniture, and makes museum-quality candlesticks and jewelry, a craft his fourteen-year-old twins are now pursuing.

We enter his house by way of a large solarium, with a raised bed of desert plants, including a desert agave, whose flowers are only supposed to bloom once every hundred years. Ramon tells us how the plant's central stalk was shooting up, growing almost a foot a day, and in the dusky light the other evening, the vertical stalk met the horizontal bar of a hanging chandelier, making a perfect cross on the wall.

I have the feeling that Ramon sees crosses everywhere, as if that classic shape were imprinted on his inner eye, keeping him focused on this central image of his faith. I feel like he's letting me in on a secret—and now I too will start seeing crosses, quite natural in Santa Fe, where the artifacts of religion have become so prevalent that every tourist shop has religious trinkets—bottle caps with glittery portraits of the Virgin Mary, silver angels blowing horns, *milagros* plastered onto mirror frames. I succumb and buy a beribboned Kar Kross. "The image of the Holy Mother facing outward is for protection from potholes and drunk drivers, facing inward—for protection from back seat drivers and bad Country Western music."

Ramon's house is warm and well loved, like everything he touches. He lets his little parakeet out of its cage, and it hops onto Donna's shoulder. "What's your name?" he asks the bird, and it answers—"Tumbleweed."

"Do you love me?" he asks, and the bird nods, *yes.*

Down a few steps into the circular living room, he shows us an *escritorio* that he made by hand, a Spanish Colonial–style writing desk held together with dovetail joints and intricately carved silverwork. When he opens the chest, there are numerous drawers, each for holding a sacred relic. The piece took him six months to complete, and though it is clearly a museum piece and could sell for some untold price, it remains a family treasure.

Back outside and behind the house, down a steep pinecone-strewn hillside, he shows us a small stone replica of his grandfather's chapel, built in dedication to his godson, Angel. The windows and door are open to the air, and often during hot summer evenings, Ramon sits here and looks all the way down to Black Mesa, a Native American holy place.

It doesn't surprise me to learn that Ramon had a passion for building forts and treehouses as a child—for isn't this another version of the

same impulse? A picture of the Holy Face of Jesus is central above the modest altar—an image that seems to go in and out of focus, hovering between the seen and unseen, a realm that Ramon naturally inhabits. Even his own visage has something of the Holy Face about it, as if he has carried this image so closely, it has become a living part of him.

But the main treasure of the place is back up the hill. Just inside the front door, I can feel Ramon hesitate, as if to build our anticipation. There to the left, on the door to his private chapel, is a large tin heart with the words *"Mio Dios"* delicately hammered. Though he never exhibits a grandiose pride despite his many accomplishments, you can tell Ramon is pleased to hear our heartfelt sounds of awe as we enter—this is truly splendid.

The *reredos*, or altar screen, is a hand-painted masterpiece, rising up along the back wall of the 33-foot-square space. It is painted in the same earthen colors Ramon collects from all over New Mexico—ochre, indigo, *amigre* red— a clay from the hills above the Santa Clara Pueblo. In his quiet, soft-spoken way, he holds back, and only hints at the mystical depths he's in touch with.

The chapel holds not only his artwork, but that of all four children as well.

Central to the high ceiling is a hand-carved, painted chandelier made by his eldest son, Leon. Besides the numerous candles, the chapel is lit by four skylights. Ramon tells us how he was up on the roof one night, and the skylights were lit from below, and he was struck by the cross shape made by the negative space, and how profound that felt, to be up there under the heavens on the roof of his own chapel and to see this cross so clearly.

In the corner of the chapel stands a statue of Our Lady of Talpas. Her altar is angled into the room with a blanket of votive candles glimmering before her. Beauty encompasses us on every side so that I feel as if I am spinning, but at the back of the room is a heavy litter that stops me—it contains the wounded body of a life-size Christ. There is something eerie about it that makes me want to turn away.

In contrast to my response, Ramon tells us about a three-year-old in the plaza, who saw this statue and stood before it for two whole hours, mesmerized. Young children, so close to the spiritual realm, seem to have a different relationship to death—it is not so horrible or gruesome.

Ramon goes on to say how he had to solicit the help of several men to help carry this *Santo Interno* the thirty-three miles to Chimayó during Holy Week. A few of the men agreed to carry the litter, but only for a short ways. "Once they began the walk," Ramon explains, "they couldn't let go." He didn't mean that they had changed their minds, but possibly their hearts were changed, for they were not only unable to leave this almost grueling procession, but literally, *physically*—their hands were not able to let go of the litter until they got it all the way to *El Santuario.* He lifts his eyebrows, a subtle indication that this account still impresses him.

There are many mysteries associated with Chimayó. Thousands walk to *El Santuario* on Good Friday, making an annual pilgrimage. Ramon tells me how he once walked in a raging blizzard—he could hardly see his hand in front of his face, but he made his way—the pain and sacrifice of such a journey not only a reflection of the pain of Christ, but an identification with His triumphant suffering.

The secrecy of the *Penitente* brotherhood is reflected in the privacy amongst the *santeros* we meet. Though these artisans have gone public, selling their carvings and paintings at the Spanish Market in Santa Fe twice a year, there is a feeling that they know more than they share. The more precious something is, the more closely it is held. When I ask Ramon why Chimayó is so important to him, he only answers, "You'll see."

Another *santero,* later in the trip, tells me that Ramon was once painting a *retablo* of a saint when he entered into another dimension, as if he went through the painting into another realm—he could even hear voices calling his name—*Ramon, Ramon, come join us,* but he knew it wasn't his time, that he had much more work to accomplish.

A life dedicated to the saints must be a saintly life; in fact even modern-day *santeros* are supposed to lead exemplary lives. As we walk around the chapel, he points out special items of interest—a beautiful hand-carved lantern with mica windows. Inside is a picture of his mother, some of her ashes in a metal bowl, as well as a dedication card that commemorates her death three years ago. He is visibly moved by the sight of it even now. Central to the altar is a painting of Christ on a standing black cross, also covered with shimmering mica.

Ramon offers us herb tea, but we opt for the Earl Grey tea bags we have tucked away in our purses. Sitting around the table, I tell him about last night's "Ultimate Margarita," too sour for some, but for me, perfection. I'm amazed when he admits that he has never tasted alcohol, not even as a teenager. He doesn't drink coffee, and he's never used tobacco either. "I'm clean," he says with a shrug. As we sip our hot tea, the parakeet hops onto my shoulder, and gives a beaky kiss to my offered cheek. Ramon asks the bird, "Do I love you?" and the bird nods, *Yes, you do.*

Holy Country

Despite Ramon's warning, I feel somewhat casual about entering *El Santuario,* but as soon as I'm through the tall wooden doors and see the green and rose altar, I am overwhelmed. The Holy Spirit can take you by surprise—like a gust of wind blowing your hat away—so the ways of the world are blown.

To the left side of the altar, we enter a room filled with crutches. There are also statues and pictures left by the faithful. People seem to have a need to leave a mark, either by giving these plaster offerings—modern-day versions of the precious *bultos* still displayed behind glass in the church, or by leaving small photos of loved ones, messages—the holy version of graffiti. A sign by the door reads: *Please light your candle, but then take it home. It gets too hot in here!*

In the next adjoining room is the famous *El Posito,* a round hole in the floor about a foot in diameter, filled with brown clay-colored earth. I drop to my knees and rub some on my forehead. I have a zip-lock baggie, to take some holy earth home to friends and family and to keep some in my own little chapel.

It is said, that back in the early 1800s, Don Bernardo Abeita was riding his horse by this spot, and saw a bright light shining from the ground. He dug down and pulled out a six-foot crucifix, which he then took to a local church, but by morning it had mysteriously returned to this hole. He repeated the action three times, and each time the crucifix returned. By then all the villag-

81

ers realized that they needed to build a chapel here on this spot, which had been sacred Indian ground at one time.

Some attribute the healing power of the place to the *Santo Niño d'Atocha*, and claim that He was the one that was discovered buried in the earth. In the trading post, *El Potrero*, next door there is so much to see—racks of books and colorful postcards, rosaries and handmade *bultos*—but a primitive lamb

fetish catches my eye. The owner claims the fetish was buried in the earth to help improve the crops. It is only an inch high, made of old white marble, and quite expensive, but I cannot resist it. I also buy a wonderful tin painting of *El Niño,* the Hispanic equivalent of the Infant of Prague. *El Niño* is always pictured sitting on a chair, wearing an agrarian version of a top hat, as well as worn-out shoes. Apparently, He has been seen walking about Chimayó at night performing small miracles, and He is always in need of shoes. An array of new ones, including tiny sneakers, are offered before His statue in another nearby *capilla,* which has the feeling of an old familiar playhouse, with precious dolls and stuffed animal friends huddled all around.

The next morning we have an appointment to meet David Ortega at his family's weaving shop, set on the edge of town. Driving our clackety-clack rent-a-car, which has picked up a rock in the hubcap, we follow him down to the old plaza nearby. Mr. Ortega holds the key to the oldest private chapel in the United States, *Oratorio de San Buenaventura del Plaza de Cerro de Chimayó,* dating back to the early seventeenth century. The *oratorio* connects to the other adobe dwellings in this crumbling, neglected plaza. Fearsome-looking dogs roam loose, barking out their masters' message, in one case written on a board set up in a driveway—*Not Welcome.*

A grey, wintry storm is approaching, and there is no electricity in the long, rectangular space. The original dirt floor has been swept clean, and though the bell rope hangs down by the door, the bell itself is frozen, as if time and song have both stopped. I begin to light votive candles, and take down the flimsy yellow curtain, hoping more natural light will enter. A charming, primitive, four-candle chandelier with a hand-carved bird hangs from the ceiling. I carefully ignite the kerosene lantern, and feel like we could be back in pioneer days with the iron potbelly stove, old wooden *vigas,* and rustic benches, each one different from the next. A rickety rail stands before the altar. There are older, precious *bultos* here as well as modern-made saints, several pictures of the *Santo Niño d'Atocha.* This little fellow gets around. Beneath one picture of the Infant of Prague I read: *The more you honor Me, the more I will bless you.* I don't know why, but it seems to be true, even with something as simple as sunlight.

As I am standing by the squat wood door, suddenly the sun comes washing in, brightening the whitewashed walls. The chapel is spare, very simple, with the special charm that only great age lends. Even the untended site has appeal, though when a local father walks by with two small children and I ask him if the boys could be in a photograph, he says firmly, "No!"

I can imagine the people who live here are tired of tourist intrusion, treating their poor plaza like a curious attraction. It seems a shame that most of the adobe dwellings, including those abutting this chapel, are being washed out, falling into complete disrepair, and the open land within, with its big beautiful poplars, is sadly overgrown. How wonderful this plaza must have been a hundred years ago, with small well-tended gardens central to the surrounding adobe dwellings. I can imagine the men and women of this village, who lived and farmed and worshipped together, frequenting their little chapel, and how close they must have felt—how the construction of the plaza itself with its connecting homes reflected this closeness. Now it is a fallen world.

Locking the front door to the *oratorio* with its heavy padlock, we are off to eleven o'clock Mass at *El Santuario,* a few miles down the road. The little five-foot-tall Portuguese priest, Father Roca, is already giving his homily as we enter. An older woman in the pew ahead of me is shivering, so I offer my jacket. She readily accepts. A young local girl sits next to me, and when we join hands for the Lord's Prayer, I notice the delicacy of her hand. It is hard to hear everything Father Roca is saying, but at one point he almost gets furious, talking about that terrible gambling casino—how men should not go there and waste their money! He even stomps his foot, and I suppress a giggle. He is as adorable as the little *Santo Niño d'Atocha.* I wonder if *He* ever stamps His small foot when He sees what goes on today.

After Mass we head for the Martinez Chapel, which is back down Route 76 toward Espanola. Micki Medina, who lives close by, tells how her father, Enemecio Ortiz Martinez, built this little chapel in 1929 with his brother Apolonio, fulfilling a promise he made during World War I. It seems that many people build small shrines or private chapels as a way of saying *Thank You* after surviving some disaster. It is a way to thank God for His gifts, a reminder that thanks can be constantly given, not just for the miraculous, but for the many small blessings.

As a girl, Micki Medina often saw her father looking out his bedroom window—"He would be staring up at his chapel praying. Just looking at it gave him even more faith." Only eight feet wide by twelve feet long, the chapel stands on top of a rugged hill in painted white purity. Two pine trunk posts stand solidly, supporting the porch and bell tower above. Certainly the construction on such a difficult site was an act of faith in itself. Micki says that the building materials were carried uphill by hand or on horseback. She adds that many devotees have climbed this steep mountain on their knees.

In 1936 a spring of water was discovered right behind the chapel. There are only a few feet of solid earth left there now before the hill slants down at a radical angle, so it seems surprising that water would come bubbling up to this height, though one can hear a rushing stream at the foot of the mountain. We are told that many people came to get water from this high holy spring for healing purposes, just as they came to *El Santuario* for earth, but even *El Posito* no longer replenishes itself, and this mythical spring has long since dried up.

Though the Martinez Chapel is dedicated to Santa Rita, saint of the impossible (she has a nasty gash on her forehead, which is actually a form of stigmata), what catches my eye is a particularly appealing statue of the Infant of Prague in soft golden yellows, cream, and green, a bit chipped and aged, probably an early plaster casting, only ten inches high, but the desire to possess it flits through my mind, and the mere notion that I could be tempted, horrifies me—What if I couldn't resist the urge? How would a stolen *bulto* affect one? Certainly not in a positive way.

I wonder if truly empowered *bultos* leave places where they do not belong, and wander away in the night like the little *Santo Niño,* wearing out his shoes. Are some soulful statues made with love and others only for money? Do the saints in heaven care about each and every statue that represents their good works? Do they mysteriously penetrate all of these statues in all of their various forms, even modern-day, machine-made ones? Isn't anything possible in the world of spirit? Isn't that the point?

That night I have a dream of a wooden *bulto* of San Isidro slowly waking and standing up before me. He is about four feet tall in the dream, larger than most statues but smaller than a man. He is very skinny and creaky, as if he has lain for so long it is difficult now to stand upright. I notice his painted beard and witness him with wariness, as if he were an apparition. When I wake I wonder why he would appear to me—What am I supposed to farm? Are the chapters of this book like different fields he means to bless? I hope so.

Donna wants to return to the Martinez Chapel at sunset, so to pass the time, we drive into Espanola and stop at another trading post, which makes me think of a line I just read in Larry Frank's book, *The Kingdom of the Saints:* "The Catholic Church is the whole world's attic . . . it is a sort of Jungian Chapel of the unconscious, a holy dreaming of sacred archetypes." Here in this store, I feel as if I've stumbled onto unearthly treasure—they have so many beautiful things. I keep circling around, going from one priceless object to another. The two old men who own the shop enjoy our enthusiasm. One of them asks me, "Are you a nun?" I have to laugh. No one's ever asked me *that* before!

Driving back to the Martinez Chapel just before sunset, we miss our turn. When I see the sign—*Every Kind of Colored Egg*—I know we have gone too far. We race back in the other direction, the light just right, golden, gleaming. Pulling in, we grab the tripod and camera bags and sprint up the hill, not wanting to miss these few precious moments, but halfway up, I can go no further—I/can/not/catch/my/breath. Claustrophobic—I throw off my coat my sweater and pull at the collar of my shirt—I cannot breathe! We both look at the gorgeous light, which is quickly passing, and finally proceed like meditative monks, walking very slowly.

We decide to return the next morning at dawn, and find ourselves on top of the mountain in semidarkness, freezing cold. The wind is whipping around the summit as we wait for the warmth of the sun. Even inside the chapel it is frigid. I didn't bring matches to light the candles, which would have quickly warmed us up. The two tall standing angels, chipped and sorrowful, hold their torches of plastic geraniums that shed no physical warmth. We peer out the window in the direction of the supposed sunrise, but a watched horizon will not yield. Turning my back to the east, I read a few entries in the notebook on the altar:

Please help me to marry the beautiful woman so I could always love her and protect her this woman completes my life and I want to always be with her. So please help me to correct my life and to treat the woman the best I can Thank You.

*

Dear God, Thank you for bringing my sister back safely from Europe. I gave you a gift. Thank you for my life and my animals, like dogs, goats, cat, horses, bird, lizerd.

*

My hope here is that for me and my mother to get back together. I know what I did wrong I shouldnt hit my mother feeling and I shouldnt have talk back and get mad at her but I wish she try to understand me what I am trying to say and to be to her. All I can say is I do really love my mother!!!!

Finally the sun makes its brilliant appearance, throwing a raspberry-colored light onto the Jemez Mountains. Dogs are barking and roosters crow. I go outside and ring the bell—*Good Morning,* to all of sleeping Chimayó.

Our Lady of Guadalupe Velarde, New Mexico

We take the back road to Taos, driving up into the mountains to Truchas and Las Trampas, where there is another beautiful church, *San José de Garcia,* dating from 1760, still maintained by local families. The massive side walls are four feet thick, which must keep it wonderfully cool in summer. Across the way there is a small store, and Donna and I each buy a tiny round pot made of special clay that contains crushed mica. The sparkly pot I choose will only hold a thimbleful of earth—so this is where I'll store my sacred dirt from *El Posito.* We are up in high pine country now at 9,000 feet. Donna sleeps as we glide down the incline to Taos to visit the pueblo there.

They also have a lovely adobe chapel with a stunning blue altar screen. Sacred corn stalks are part of the painted design on either side of the altar. Outside, an old woman selling jewelry tells me, "We are all Catholic here." Past history seems to have fallen away, while the teenagers that hang out by the split rail fence near the cross-filled cemetery look resentful and self-conscious.

I am impressed that there is not one single TV aerial in sight, but then I discover that there is no electricity at all. "Our elders would not allow for it," the old woman tells me. You can feel the tranquility, the subtle difference when electricity is not sizzling through wire, pumping out radio music and harsh light. Here in this magnificent location, beneath the snow-capped mountains, over two hundred people live within this multi-layered structure, ingenious precursor to our modern-day condos. Still, there is something sad about this ancient, dignified culture being on display.

It is a short visit, because we want to get to Eulogio and Zoraida Ortega's in Velarde this afternoon. I have spoken to Eulogio on the phone (his name, quite appropriately, means eulogy), and I have nothing but high praise and commendation for him and his seventy-nine year old wife, Zoraida.

Their medium-sized chapel, twelve feet by twenty-four, is set at the edge of a large apple orchard, the entrance surrounded by climbing roses. Inside, Eulogio points out that the benches have been moved against the walls, be-

cause a group of *Penitentes* came to pray the rosary the other day, and they like to kneel on the hard wood floor. Zoraida, who is a weaver of Rio Grande textiles, spent a year creating the *reredos* behind the altar. It is exceptional. Eulogio says that when she was painting the decorative designs down by the floor, he brought in a mattress so that she could be comfortable as she worked.

Their marriage of fifty-four years could be an inspiration to all of us in our struggling states of couplehood, pushing and pulling. Together they were happily surprised last summer to receive the Masters Award for Lifetime Achievement, presented by the Spanish Market in Santa Fe.

Back in the corner of the chapel, I am drawn to the collection of crosses by the antique stove. Eulogio has developed a reputation not only for his soulful *bultos,* but for his wooden crucifixes as well. A particularly fine one, in perfect proportion to the room, is central to the altar. Eulogio has donated crucifixes to churches as well as to small *capillas* in the Pecos River Valley, but inside the house there is a virtual museum of carvings.

Entering their comfortable pine-paneled house through a curved sun room, where Zoraida paints the *bultos* that her husband carves out in his rustic studio, we sit around the table eating Fritos pie and tamales. I feel a certain ease and serenity here, so at home I could curl up on the sofa and fall asleep as they continue to tell us stories.

Marketing apples in northern New Mexico, the two of them noticed a chapel with an empty belfry, and then discovered the bell lying in a sheep field nearby. The farmer accepted seven bushels of apples in trade, and Eulogio and Zoraida were very pleased, for the bell, cast in St. Louis a hundred years ago, had perfect tone.

As Eulogio says, "You know we've gotten visitors from almost every European country. Even the curator from the Prague Museum was here. Visitors from almost every state of the union. We get groups, and sometimes someone just shows up. That's sort of our *fate,* I tell Zoraida."

"Faith?" I ask.

"Bringing people into our home. It has really transformed our lives."

While Zoraida carries herself somewhat protectively, having undergone three cancer operations, and most recently the removal of a diseased kidney, Eulogio seems quite relaxed in his body, though he admits that he has heart disease and doesn't know if he will live much longer. This seems shocking news, as this saintly man looks the vision of health, with such a mild and pleasant manner, you can't imagine anything going wrong for him. But when Zoraida serves up some of her apple pie, it is so mouth-

watering I have to ask her if the crust is made with lard, and she goes, *"Shh,"* nodding, and whispering *yes*—"But it's not good for Eulogio's heart."

I wonder when he first started carving *bultos,* and he says that he began when he retired. He was a principal of a small elementary school in Dixon. "I

read in the local paper that someone had stolen a carving from *El Santuario de Chimayó.* As you go in on the left, they have a beautiful carving of San Rafael, made by one of the most famous carvers who lived in the seventeenth century, José Rafael Aragon. And somebody stole it. A picture of it came in the local paper, and they were offering a reward of five hundred dollars for its return. I felt so bad, I thought, why don't I try and carve one, and so I began. But then some little girl brought it back. She said that she found it in the dump! Ours is now in our chapel, holding up his little fish. You saw it.

"But after that I just kept going. I knew I could do it, because that was my major in college, art. I like carving, because I forget everything. When you start carving, it's like eating piñon, you just keep going and going. I think it's a form of prayer, sometimes.

"But the chapel was Zoraida's idea," he adds. Eulogio explains that after his wife's first operation, she wanted to build a chapel to Our Lady of Guadalupe—"She believes the Divine Mother answered her prayers and gave her back her health."

"So when you pray, do you pray to her?" I ask Zoraida.

"Oh yeah," she nods. She goes on to tease her husband, saying how Eulogio thought a chapel would be too much work.

"At first I thought, maybe a little grotto, you know. But that wasn't good enough for Zoraida. And then these boys from Mexico showed up looking for work, and this one big guy with great big hands said he did this work in Mexico. Zoraida said to me—'So there you go.' They helped me with the foundation and walls, and then I did the rest. We had to bring in the adobes."

But Eulogio doesn't always go to the chapel to pray. He likes to get up at four o'clock in the morning and then sits in his special chair in the living room and reads from the bible he was given during World War I. "I have a standard prayer," he says. "*Blessed be God. Blessed be His Holy Name. Blessed be Jesus Christ through God and through Man. Blessed be the name of Jesus. Blessed be His most Sacred Heart . . .* Are you a Catholic?" he asks me.

I tell him I am, but only recently.

"Generally converts make better Catholics," he smiles. Zoraida was also a convert. She grew up a Methodist, and went to a Methodist boarding school. They got married in the Methodist Church.

Thomas Merton's book *Seeds of Contemplation* is there on the table—it is one of Eulogio's favorites. Thomas Merton also converted to Catholicism, Eulogio reminds me. I was under the impression that Merton had abandoned his faith toward the end of his life in favor of Buddhism, but Eulogio says, "No, he was just interested in the eastern religions, so he went to see the Dalai Lama."

Eulogio says that Thomas Merton was in Indonesia, on his way back to Kentucky, where he lived in a hermitage on the grounds of his monastery, when he was electrocuted in his bathroom. Death is on Eulogio's mind, though he does not seem fearful. He likes to say that he is eighty years old, but Zoraida reminds him that he is not eighty yet. He will be eighty on Holy Innocents Day, the 28th of December. "You know the Holy Innocents," he reminds us—"that's when Herod killed all those children. He wanted to kill the baby Jesus, and that's my birthday!"

Opening a rare edition of *The Hound of Heaven,* he begins to read the poem out loud, but then he stops and adds—"When I came out of the army, I was an agnostic. But the Hound of Heaven got after me!"

We talk about St. Thérèse, The Little Flower, and I show him photos of our chapel in progress, dedicated to her Little Way. He says, "You know, just last week, on October 19th, she was made a Doctor of the Church." I knew this was going to happen, but I am surprised by the date—my son Ayler's birthday. Now the day will be doubly blessed.

My friend Pedro Leitau drove all the way from Paris to Lisieux in Normandy, trying to find me a statue of Thérèse for the chapel, but to no avail. Later I find out that a Berkshire friend, Chris Bamford, ended up avoiding Assisi because of the earthquake, and went to Rome instead, where he happened to go to St. Peter's on the very day that the Pope was declaring St. Thérèse a Doctor of the Church. With over 100,000 people, priests were scattered throughout the huge crowd, serving communion. Carmelites from all over the world were throwing rose petals up into the air. There were roses strewn all over the steps of the great Basilica, with the image of this little girl on a giant banner, there for all to see.

I ask Eulogio if he might be able to carve me a *bulto* of St. Thérèse for my chapel, and he says that he cannot promise. He has difficulty working in the winter now. He's not in it for the business, as he doesn't like to deal with money very much. He thinks some of the *santeros* are charging exorbitant prices, and he has a strange feeling about that.

"We've sort of slowed down," Zoraida explains. "We're not doing as much work as we used to."

"We're doing more praying now!" Eulogio laughs. It is a joy to laugh along with him.

Sandstone Cathedral Espanola, New Mexico

In the heart of mythic New Mexico, we take a right on Route 183 toward Ojo Caliente, known for its curative waters. Halfway there, we see the welcoming arch of *Rancho de San Juan,* a discreet but luxurious country inn surrounded by mountainous terrain where the sandstone cathedral is hidden. You do not need to stay at this exclusive *Relais & Chateaux* hotel in order to see the shrine. Five dollars buys you a key, and though this might discourage some explorers, the experience far exceeds the price.

Ra Paulette is waiting for us—a handsome, sun-tanned, wiry man with luminous blue-green eyes. He is probably only 5'7" but as far as I am concerned, he is a giant, for he has mastered a mountain. Calm, speaking in a humble fashion, he lets John Johnson and David Heath, the owners, explain their role in the project.

"A month after the inn opened, in June of 1994, Ra came walking down the steps. He was wearing this big Panama hat and Hawaiian print shorts," John says, "and I looked at my partner and asked—Do we have anybody checking in today, and he said, 'No.' So who is this character?"

"Your local door-to-door cave salesman," Ra puts in. "I saw the spot and the possibility right away. It was high. Visually, it wasn't in direct eye contact, and there was a good ravine for the tailings pile." It is interesting to note that a tailings pile increases three times in volume when it comes out of the solid, compacted interior.

Ra's first hand-carved shrine, called *The Heart Chamber,* was set two

93

miles back on public land. At first he liked the idea of no private ownership. He only told a few people about it, because for him this underground chamber was a retreat, a place for renewal, but word got out, and then hundreds of people began to make a pilgrimage to this soulful excavation.

Visitors often left mementos within the cavernous space, just as they might at a more traditional shrine, leaving a little part of themselves—photos of loved ones, candles and prayers, messages scribbled on paper, significant objects. Ra feels that this is part of what it's all about. "Leaving objects is an expression of openheartedness, connecting oneself to a place." Surely, there are negative ways of doing the same thing—scribbling obscenities or defacing a wall with graffiti, even posting No Trespassing signs. "People who feel minimized, people who feel insignificant want to make a mark that is territorial—they want to claim it for themselves, and that is a very different thing."

But Ra had chosen a piece of land that was not his own, and there was no way to control it. Too many people wanted admittance, and the crumbly sandstone earth was unable to withstand the traffic. Local officials became so concerned that Ra decided to fill *The Heart Chamber* back in with its original tailings.

This seems disturbing—like razing a beautiful building, or burying something alive, but perhaps it was more akin to what the Egyptians did with their pyramids. Or as Ra explains it—"The tide just came back in."

In any case, he wanted to make sure that his next location would be safer, more private, that access would be open, but somewhat limited, for the sandstone material he works with is fragile, and cannot take much abuse.

As we walk up the path to Ra's new creation, *Windows in the Earth,* we are hardly aware of the cathedral waiting within the eccentrically shaped sandstone hoodoo. I only realize that we have arrived when I see several discreet, elongated oval windows set into the face of the mountain. Following the trail around to the side, we find a glass door, and with key in hand, we let ourselves in.

I have never seen anything like this. The huge multiple arching curves of the ceiling follow the grain of the sandstone, creating beautiful swirls that you want to touch, though the heights are well out of reach. It looks very smooth, as if he used a power sander, but I know that there is no electricity up here and that he pulled the earth out bit by bit with very basic hand tools. No wonder he has been called "the human back-hoe."

At every angle a new surprise opens before us—it is like walking into an opening flower—you want to lie down in the big billowing hammock-like space and be gently swung back and forth. The morning light is lovely, subdued. We are glad we came early, that we have the place to ourselves, but as usual, we have too much stuff—extra layers of clothes, two camera bags, a tripod, water, purses. I also have a sack of votive candles as well as Donna's newly purchased wooden cross, stuck down into my belt.

Though this is not specifically a Christian shrine, we set the cross to the side of the throne altar, above the central open area, which was designed for performance and ceremony. They have had several weddings here, as well as vow renewals, drummings, chantings, and concerts. I imagine how spectacular it would be inside here during a full moon at the height of summer.

Clustering candles on small mirror platforms embedded into the sandstone walls, the carved designs around the niches flare like bursts of flame, while the mirrored surfaces resemble water. One altar appears to be a fountain carved miraculously out of seafoam, sacred pools spilling from one to another. The mirrors not only lend a feeling of liquidity, but also double the

carved image above—creating a kind of disorientation, or spacelessness, which is exactly what Paulette must have intended when he dreamed up the Luminous Egg Chamber.

The chamber is small, only meant for one, though it feels expansive—a perceptual dichotomy. "When your mind tells you one thing, and your perceptual reality tells you another, you get stretched out in the middle and interesting things start to happen." A hole of light enters at the top of the chamber and descends, enveloping one in a fog of light—this may be as close as one can get to a prenatal experience of the womb.

I ask Ra what it was like to stand facing a mountain, and then to enter, and he admits it was like going into a woman's body. "I felt like a puppy worming my way to the nipple," he says, and indeed the curves and undulations here are very feminine. There is hardly a straight line in the place. I am reminded of water surging and falling, fire flaming upwards, the curl of shell or the earth's upheaval, all the elements at once in motion—yet caught in a volcanic flash.

With so much visual activity, it seems odd that the space is so restful. I sit down on one of the many benches sculpted into the walls, offering a view of the Jemez Mountains. Around another corner is a writer's nook, with cherry desktop and wooden bookshelves embedded in the sandstone, as if it were somebody's study. A notebook rests on the desk here beneath a portal window, and I page through:

> Author of all life
> Spirit of Wisdom
> Come forward in this stone temple
> and anchor my heart
> deep into the earth
> Allow me to reach into the heavens
> and know God
> for his magnificence and Peace.
>
> *
>
> We came from Arabia to be amazed!
> Ra, to be at one with the sky, clouds and earth, provides the soul with a
> privileged glimpse into the past where man had a healthier perspective on
> our beautiful land. Thank you for such an honor.
>
> *
>
> Our Mother who Art Within Us
> we celebrate your many names
> your wisdom come, your will be done
> unfolding from the depths of us
> each day you give us all we need
> you remind us of our limits and we let go
> you support us in our power, and we act with courage
> for you are the dwelling place within us

the power around us and the celebration among us
as it was in the beginning
so shall it be now.

I think of what fun this place would be for a child, exploring these magical chambers, crawling in and all around, how it's also the kind of secret place that the child within each of us craves. While working here, Paulette himself must have gone back into some childhood world of pretend, where you are so much in the moment, everything else falls away. We agree that play and spirituality are very close, play and wonder, play and awe.

Certainly nothing was prefigured in the making of this sandstone cathedral. The mountain itself instructed him, the way a piece of wood often dictates the shape of a hand-carved *bulto*. If one trusts in the material, it will lead, it will give direction. One can feel that spontaneity here, no way of planning this out on a graph or computer. It is too random, too fanciful.

Small stones plucked from the local terrain have a lovely haphazard quality, embedded like jewels in their sandstone setting. I enjoy seeing the footprints of other visitors in the sandy floor—somehow it reminds me of our transience, seeing the tracks of our predecessors, realizing that this was once a hard, clean-swept surface, slowly transforming itself back into sand.

Ra goes on to say that he would like to carve a tree of life shrine. "The main column, in the center of the room, would be the trunk, all carved out of sandstone, and the branches would umbrella out over the ceiling. I'd like to carve a female figure somewhere in it, or on it, or around it—The Mama."

This seems to be a recurrent theme—how men and women both are trying to connect to the Great Feminine, whether it be the Holy Mother, or what Gabriel Cousens calls *Shekinah* energy, Kali, Tara, Kuan-Yin, Our Lady of Guadalupe, or the Great Earth Mother. In all her various forms, she seems to be appearing wherever we go, asking and offering Her Love.

As Ra worked here, he not only carried his tools to the site, but also hauled thousands of pounds of birdseed, which he sprinkled over the top of the hoodoo—imagining that all that flutter would somehow protect him and hold this petrified sand dune up. As he worked, he hung a sign around his neck—*If this structure crushes me, it's my own fault. I'm sorry to put whoever comes after my body into danger.* The cremated ashes of his father's remains were spread on top of the mountain, and though he had a rather conflicted relationship there, it is clear that he's glad they have that connection.

With Ra working five or six hours a day, *Windows in the Earth* took a couple of years to finish, but still the work goes on. He is here today to wash the windows and to pick up the place. "I feel responsible. An untended space can easily fall into disrepair. I have a part of me that's much funkier, but the owners are afraid that the mess is going to spread." There is one small niche where a clutter of things have accumulated—a miniature bible, a sand dollar, a photograph of a Hindu teacher's feet strewn with flowers, a shell, a toy, a lipstick kiss on paper, spare change. "I'm into the quarters," he admits. "They're handy in the laundromat."

I have to admit to wedging a tiny *milagro* man back into the seam of a sunburst carving—I too want to be connected to this place. Outside, hikers have made their totem offerings along the path, stacking piles of stones as a form of response.

We talk about the difference of turning a shrine over to the world, letting visitors do what they will, and continuing to exert some control over the space. There are clearly two mindsets on this: one is that whatever people leave behind becomes part of the shrine's transforming life—it continues to evolve; but I tend to agree with the owners here—the uncluttered purity of the space is important.

Perhaps thinking of the cleaning ahead of him, Ra mentions that each of the windows is made up of three different panes of glass. It would have been too heavy and awkward to fit ten-foot-high ovals into the walls. The sandstone material does not allow for large horizontal spaces, so the rooms and windows are very vertical, and the arches unfold in a harmonious series of tall curves.

While he was alone, working in the earth, he asked himself a lot of questions—*Why is this all here? What is it here for?* "Life has created this potentiality to be aware of the sacred—and something in us has to be thankful. Something has to sense wonder. There has to be an instrument for sensing beauty. The whole idea of sacredness is in our relationship to things," not simply a system of belief, but an activity.

Ra says that he was very connected to the hollowness of this space, to the emptiness of it. "All of this came out piece by piece, and I touched every bit of it. As I got closer to the existing walls, I had to become more and more careful. Closer to the walls, the energy is more refined, more sensitive, more feminine."

Ra and his wife live together in a yurt in the little town of Embudo. After a period of separation, he is feeling the pressure to make money. In the past he did exactly what he wanted to do without regard for finance, but that can be difficult on a marriage. "I would have done all of this for nothing," Ra admits, "but now I can't afford to. It's hard to promote yourself when you want to do the actual work. We associate creativity with the person doing it, and all of a sudden it becomes personality worship." I think of Georgia O'Keefe, and how she, as a reclusive artist in nearby Abiqui, would have shunned the popularity that has made her extraordinary life and work almost commonplace.

"Art is not getting into the heart of our lives, because we use it to make money, to run galleries, to run institutions, and it is antithetical to the creative spirit, which is coming from some place beyond ourselves. We can get credit— we bring our technique, our expertise—we bring everything that we are and give everything we have to that moment, but only if there is grace will magical things start to happen."

Little Rose Chapel Underway

More and more people are being drawn into this project. We meet a blacksmith, William Trowbridge, from Sharon, Connecticut, who is eager to participate. He will make the large strap hinges for the door. Pete Shepley agrees to drive with me down to Connecticut to look for chestnut boards. Pete will help Mason build the form for the barrel vault. He also helps us find a beautiful escutcheon and door handle that will harmonize with William's metal work, an unpainted iron finish that looks very old.

It's amazing the amount of time and decision making that goes into thinking through the mechanics of a door—how it will open with the foot-thick wall, how it will hinge, if it will swing in or out, if it will be placed flush with the exterior wall or the interior wall, how that will affect the strap hinges, on and on, until finally everyone agrees, and the project moves forward.

My friend Kate Knapp brings me a stack of books on stained-glass window design, but most of it looks too modern for my taste. There is one book that has reproductions of cathedral windows, and I find a small detail from a French cathedral, and blow it up on the color Xerox machine until it is 18 × 24 inches. The design pictures an abstract flower with many petal pieces. Kate's boyfriend, Michael Magnotti, thinks he can reproduce it, though it is a complicated design. Together we go to the glass store in West Stockbridge, and find beautiful shimmering Tiffany-like glass, golden yellow and pink with butterfly surfaces that turn to lavender and blue-green in certain lights.

Weeks later, I drop by their house, a bit apprehensive. Will I like it? And what if I don't? The cut pieces are all laid out, not yet fastened. When Michael turns on the light table, I am in awe—it is even more beautiful than I could have imagined—perfectly luscious. Usually a commissioned work can't live up to the vague splendor of the imagination. But this exceeds it.

At an antique store in South Egremont I find two Chinese chairs that look like thrones. Placed together, they connect to make a nice comfortable seat for two. But Mason isn't sure about the chairs. He had something more modest in mind. I remind him that he is in charge of the exterior, and I am supposed to be in charge of the interior—a hard line to draw when he is doing so much, but I want to defend my territory. When I ask him to help me carry the chairs out to the chapel, which now has plywood walls, awaiting the fieldstone masonry, he is resistant.

Just because we are building a chapel doesn't mean there are no frustrations. I find myself getting angry—he never seems to like anything I initiate, and I resent it. I don't interfere with his projects. But I don't like the tone of my resentment either, especially here on the site of this sacred place. Why does everything always seem like a power struggle? Should I back down, return the chairs, which I have taken on approval? He finally says he thinks they're fine, just not what he would have chosen.

My father is about to arrive for a visit, and I am very worried about him. Calling Dr. Fritz, I find out that my father checked himself into the Oconomowoc Hospital over the weekend because he was having chest pains. "They took an X-ray and saw a dark spot," the doctor tells me. As soon as I hear that I burst into tears.

"Then there's nothing more we can do," I cry, assuming the cancer is spreading. I know that Dad cannot tolerate any more chemical therapy, and he's too weak for another operation. I apologize for my tears, but Dr. Fritz says that it's all right. He's used to it. "We'll give him a CAT scan when he returns from his trip. Just give him a really good time," as if it were my last opportunity.

My brother David drives Dad from Logan Airport, and by the time they arrive, Dad looks wasted, emaciated, not well. We are all very concerned. He has lost so much weight and can barely eat. He goes to bed as soon as he arrives, and sleeps until dinner and then only picks at his food, saying, "I know something is wrong with me. I'm just not well." No one wants to think about the possibility of spreading cancer.

The one exciting bit of news we receive over dinner is that my brother is going to finally get remarried this weekend, a small private ceremony on a boat off Cape Cod with just their two daughters from previous marriages. Dad won-

ders if we shouldn't fly down, but we all agree, it would be too much exertion. What he needs now is quiet and rest.

I tell him that I plan on feeding him tiny meals every two hours, but he should only eat what he wants. I am not going to force-feed. This week is devoted to doing just what he wants to do. I will make suggestions, but he will make all the final decisions. This is an attitude he can live with. He is grateful for the massages and foot reflexology sessions I've lined up, and within days he looks as if someone has watered his flower and he is quickly springing back to life. His color and mood are better. He loves the guest room. He loves the comfortable queen-size bed. He couldn't be happier. He still sleeps a lot, and eats very little, but he is a joy to have around.

On the third day, Dad even goes so far as to take a short ride with me, cantering Nashotah around the ring. But afterwards, he is exhausted, and quickly retreats to bed. When he is up and awake, I keep giving him tiny nibbles of food, a slice of avocado with oil and vinegar, a cherry tomato with mayo, cheese on a cracker, a cup of soup, but he always feels full no matter how little he eats, and he continues to complain of severe stomach pain. He believes he may have ulcers.

This disturbs me, because he had cancerous ulcers in his esophagus, and even though the esophagus has been removed, there was also some cancer in his lymph nodes. Mason discovers over the Internet that that there is only a five percent survival rate with esophageal carcinoma, which is a statistic I don't need to hear. I keep lighting candles, praying.

My brother David, always the humorist, calls on the morning of his wedding and leaves this message—"Father, I know not what I do." He has organized a way for us to partake in the ceremony—over a cell phone! My niece Isabelle holds the receiver, while Mason, Dad, and I are each on a different outlet. The service is short, but still I am moved for my brother long-distance. We take a bottle of champagne out to our little just-begun chapel and christen the event with champagne flutes full, drinking to the newlyweds in the warm afternoon light. How nicely the brain is dazzled. I feel very happy, and know my father is pleased, for now the deed is done.

On Sunday, Dad agrees to come to church with me, and Father Russo gives one of his best homilies, about the difference between acting from a set of rules and acting from the heart as a Christian. Dad enjoys the homily and even takes communion. He especially likes seeing all the children up by the altar at the end of the service. Outside, we have a chat with Father Russo. Dad tells him that our family is Episcopalian, "We are descendants of Henry the VIII," he proclaims, and Father Russo counters with the number of Masses Henry paid for at his *death to take care of his time in purgatory—"That's how Protestant he was!" But all is good-natured.*

We drive on to Hillsdale, and stop at Aubergine to get some soup. Dad mainly wants to drink soup. Knowing my father's condition, David Lawton, the chef, refuses to charge me for the delicious chicken broth and mushroom soup he's made. We go home and have a heavenly outdoor repast beneath the wisteria vines. Despite the pain, Dad is happy here, looking out at the rolling Berkshire Hills.

On Tuesday morning I drive my father back to Boston. He tells me funny stories from his childhood—how he had a pet spider monkey one summer, but by the end of August he came to the conclusion that there was more to life than taking care of a pet monkey. He was such a strange child he even liked taking his castor oil. Going from laughter to tears, Dad mourns Princess Diana's untimely death, "I know it's not normal to be so emotional." He keeps thinking of her dying at the height of her youth and fame and beauty, how she will never grow old.

Dad doesn't want me to wait with him at the airport, so after we park, check his bags, and walk out to the gate, I give him a hug good-bye and leave him there by the magazine stand. Walking away, I get choked up—Will I ever see my wonderful, loving father again?

Jeff Albert begins gathering stone—a most generous gift from our neighbor's wall. He places the first stones down on the foundation, and quickly, very quickly the sides go up. Suddenly we realize, we have a lot to get together. The stone nicho *we've been waiting for has just arrived, but getting it home is no easy chore. It takes all three Mexican workers, heaving and straining, to lower it onto the truck bed. Jeff Albert forklifts the pallet off the truck, and the three of us, grunting and groaning, get it into position between the other two niches.*

The tumbled-marble floor arrives, and with the help of the trucker we unload box after box from the back of his truck. Everyone is intrigued that we are building a chapel. They want to know all about it. None of the tiles seem to have broken, which is amazing, since they came in orange crates all the way from Italy with only the flimsiest packing material.

Mason tapes out an 8 × 13 foot area on the garage floor, and we lay out the tiles in the pattern we've designed, a row of 4 inch squares on the outside, then 1 × 4 inch bars separated by 1 inch plugs, forming a border around the basket-weave mosaic strip, with the 6 inch squares set diagonally, filling the center. A large mosaic dove holding an olive branch will be in front of the altar, surrounded by smaller stones. The marble is the color of mother's milk, deliciously smooth.

Mason wants to begin cutting the tiles right away, and I have to hold him back. I say there are variables we can't foresee, such as the depth of the altar. Better not to get ahead of ourselves. I am beginning to see a basic difference in the way we work. He wants everything planned out ahead of time. Using his computer and working with the model helps him to envision the space, while I want to wait and act in the moment, see how things will look as they are going in. Our methods complement each other—if we step back and let them—as long as neither of us gets too rigid or too loose.

I am on the phone constantly with my brothers and sister, talking about our father's health. He has been having severe stomach pains, and needs more medication. They have not yet received the results of the latest CAT scan, but Dr. Fritz thinks it's too early for the cancer to return in his stomach after radiation treatment. It is so hard to wait. To hear one little scrap of good news, only to worry about the next thing.

The stone walls of the chapel are going up beautifully. I really like Jeff Albert's sensibility, though I keep urging him to use more rounded stones. Mason and I walk out to the neighboring wall and cull a few stones we like. I find a small one that is solid pink quartz. Even with all we are taking, the stone wall hardly looks altered.

As we reach the appropriate height, the holy water font is set into the masonry, and looks so beautiful. We're getting day after day of perfect Indian summer weather. The only problem is too little rain. The pond is sinking, and wells are drying up, but strangely, the holy water font is full.

Another week passes, and my father continues to lose pound after pound. I call Dr. Fritz's office again, and Lisa, his assistant, says she'll call back when she knows anything.

Later that afternoon, I receive her call, and she says, "Good news! Your father's blood work looks perfect. Dr. Armand went down into his stomach and saw two gastric ulcers, a reaction to the radiation, but they were not cancerous. No signs of cancer anywhere!"

As soon as I hang up, I burst out crying. I go out onto the deck, sit down in a chair and simply weep, tears of gratefulness, tears of relief. All I can think of is—Thank you, thank you, thank you, thank you. Has there ever been a warmer or more balmy day?

PART THREE

Be Blessed, Deep South

Dear Jesus Give Me Money,
For I have None.

> Love, Bill
> Post-it Prayer

Erzulie's Altar, Voodoo Spiritual Temple

(*previous page*)
Hermon Dennis with his Book of Sermons

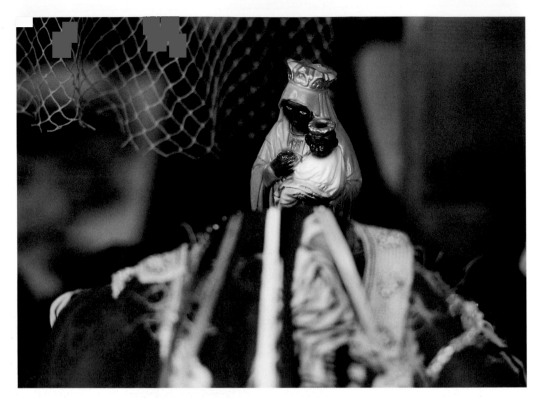

Black Madonna/
Flamingo Head
with Heart, Voodoo
Spiritual Temple

Yancy Chapel

Our Lady of Blind River

Noonie Smith's Memorial Chapel

MARGARET AND HERMON DENNIS

All Is Welcome Temple Vicksburg, Mississippi

Up against the red and white Lego-looking fortress of Margaret's Grocery, the *Coca-Cola* sign blends right in. Coke was first bottled here in Vicksburg, "the red carpet city," known for its southern hospitality, but surely they didn't roll one out for the Union Army in 1863. Despite the Civil War consciousness of citizens here, I am surprised that the local Court House Museum still displays a KKK mask with this inscription: *To Northerners the KKK was an evil organization, designed to intimidate and control former slaves . . . but to Southerners, the Klan became a means of restoring some semblance of order and decency.*

Five miles north of downtown Vicksburg, in a poor neighborhood of rundown trailers the locals call simply "Kings," you cannot miss the colorful turrets and towers that leap up around Margaret's grocery store. Vicksburg officials refused to give Hermon Dennis a permit to finish building his "upper room" prayer tower. It does look rickety, but he still wants to finish it so that sinners from Jackson can come over and pray. "I answer to God, not the city."

An old plywood sign with the exclamation ALL IS WELCOME JEWS AND GENTILES has begun to peel, victim to the elements. Though many of the hand-painted messages outside are almost indecipherable, inside God's message is still delivered loud and clear by Reverend Hermon Dennis: "God sent down an angel, because He wanted me to tell the world that He Loves You. We got to love *Him*. We are given shades of skin for a bouquet of flowers.

107

Everything He made He made a different color, right? Don' know a black hen egg from a white hen egg, do you, when you buying it in the store? Don' know a black cow milk from a white cow milk. God works in bouquets. All different colors mixed together. He gives us so much, but we're too busy not getting along, too busy not respecting one another. Respect and love, that's the sermon I preach. We're all the same in God's eyes."

When Margaret was widowed in her late sixties, Hermon told her if she would marry him, he would turn her brown-plank family grocery into a holy temple. He lived up to his promise. And Margaret loves it, sitting in her metal rocker, eating fried chicken with a Sunday friend. But I am overwhelmed, as if I'd been set on an inner limb of a Christmas tree, ornaments and music all around, an amazing array of junk turned jewel-like. Every inch of this long narrow room is absolutely crammed, wavy wooden trim hammered on the ceiling in sunburst patterns, laundry detergent caps smattered over surfaces, tinsel ribbon, twinkling lights. What is welcome on this altar? Everything! For Spirit permeates the world. Cast-off trash has been admitted to the sacred. *Hallelujah.* Throw-away stuff has suddenly become splendid, richer than the downtown mansions where waxed antiques boast their antebellum heritage. This is a junkyard heaven, and we are getting there by way of a bus.

Reverend Hermon takes me back outside to his silver spray-painted school-bus chapel. *Rosa Parks where are you?* Don't get up! Hermon has a great big "manuscript" of sermons, each page covered with plastic and scribbled with code. It looks like it belongs in the Smithsonian, not just as a curiosity, but because it is a genuine article of religious folk art. Though locals might discredit him, and one newspaper article called him "a ridiculous man," his memory is good, quoting chapter and verse. He comes out of an oral tradition, his sermons like lyrics practically sung, punctuated by wild gesticulations, a kick of a leg or a stomp and a *Whoop*—"GLORY, Hallelujah!" There is no shame over praising here. No self-consciousness. Only the Holy Spirit alive and well in Vicksburg, Mississippi.

"Yo' womens were the first preachers, after Jesus Christ rose. Men don't want to give you credit for it, but Mary Magdalene was the first one saw Jesus Christ when he rose that morning. Mary Magdalene carry the message—*Go and tell them that I am alive!* You was the first preacher. You smarter than a man. God done given it to you, but you not exercising it."

This bible class bus is also decorated to the hilt. It might not roll, but it can fly. The covered seats are ready pews. Hermon is up by the steering wheel, where he has erected a pulpit. "My life is more than you could learn about if you were to be here one year." To make up for lost time he begins at the beginning. "Six long days nobody knew I was born, cause my father was over at his girlfriend's house, and my mother died at birth. People for blocks could smell the odor. When people broke in, there my mother layin' dead, and I was just out of her womb. The doctor said, 'That child can't possibly live. He ain't

had no nursin', no food, his navel not even been cut. He going to die tonight.' But I had a praying grandmother. She said, 'I know The Man! That's all I know, because I was born in slavery.' She was twelve years old when they declared war. But she know The Man, and she was determined to raise me.

"When I was two year old, a storm took me right out of an old lady's arms—this tornado was pickin' up everything, and it carried me across the river of Mississippi, but God was up there with me. It was God that held me in the hollow of His hand. And when He let me down, I was swinging on a wire fence by my trousers, and they say I was laughin', just two years old."

Hermon has always been God's Baby. When his grandmother died, he had to go live with his father, an unhappy experience that lasted only a year before he ran off. " I was sleeping under a tree scared to death of my father. He was dangerous, and he beat me to death. I pass a whitey man pecan orchard. He has his arm folded, and I say, 'Captain, can I pick up a few pecans?' And he said yes, but instead of puttin' 'em in my pocket, I put 'em in my mouth, hull and all.

"He said, 'Boy, can you work?' I say, *'Yahsir, yahsir, yahsir.'* 'Quit saying, Yes Sir,' the whitey man told me. But my grandmother taught me to say Yes Sir and No Sir. My grandmother taught me to say Yes Ma'am to you. She taught me to tip my hat to a lady when I meet her. Old folks used to do that, but it's the devil ruling the world today. After the war was over, everybody decided to make money and forgot about God Almighty, but I have never forgot it.

"'Boy, can you pick cotton?' 'I can pick three-four hundred pound a day. I been in the fields *all* my life.' 'Can you *shuck* cotton?' 'I can do it all. I can do everything for a farm, better than you can. Black folks know how to farm.'

"'Boy? Do you want to stay with us?' But I say, 'My Daddy's looking for me right now. I got to get 100 miles away from my Daddy. He's a dangerous man.' 'Boy, do you *believe,* I'm going to repeat, do you *believe* that your Daddy will come on a white man's place and take you away if you don't want to?'

"So, he persuaded me to come on up to the mansion. Seventeen, eighteen room, beautiful mansion. He say, 'Boy I'd like to raise you. Is you willing to be called a black sheep?' I say, '*Yahsir*. I glad to be called a black sheep. Anything you call me, I'm glad for you to call it.'

"'Boy, what kinds of boy *is* you?'"

When Mr. Hinds, the plantation owner, took Hermon home, Mrs. Hinds taught him at night because he couldn't go to the white school. "The others call me ape, an' monkey, nigger an' fool, everything you could think of, and you know what I done? *Smile.* My grandmother didn't teach me to get mad. She taught me to Love You! Nothing hurt you but a lick. I did not depart from her training.

"People would ask Mr. Hinds, 'What you doin' with that black nigger?' And Mr. Hinds would tell them, 'This isn't a black nigger. This is a black sheep in the family.' *Glory Hallelujah*!"

Hermon stayed with the Hindses until he was twenty-six years old and joined the army. "The devil try to get rid of me *many times.* I went through the army, back there in the forties, in the South Pacific, fighting the Japanese. Thirty days on water from New York City, we run into the Japanese fleet. The captain and the general say, that young soldier there, he been preaching ever since he board this ship. Get him down here in the hatch. So I go down with my little group and we pray. Bombs fell round like showers of rain. But bombs didn't go off."

Other people's ridicule doesn't bother Hermon. Police came to his house early one morning, and asked Margaret for him to come out. "Preacher, you know those ten commandments you were talking about? God done give 'em to you, but we found the tablets. We gonna tell you where they at. You go right now and get 'em, and when you get 'em, you bring 'em down to the police station, and you let all the police lay their hands on 'em. And then you take

'em to the sheriff's department, to the jailhouse, and let all those in jail lay their hands on 'em. And then you take 'em out to the business stores where you been doing business—where they been laughing at you for years—they say you're crazy but we know you're not."

"So I went and found 'em where God had 'em stored for me, stacked away."

I ask Hermon where they were, but he responds, "God ain't told me to tell you that!"

Following his vision as much as any spiritual, outsider artist, Hermon even built his own Ark of the Covenant, a plastic footlocker spray-painted gold, lined with plush satin to cradle the tablets, protected by an intricate set of mazes and locks as well as an interior glass doorknob. "Don't give me no credit. Give God the credit for what been done here. You not lookin' at nothing that I done. You lookin' what God done through me in my hands.

Nothin' that I want credit for. I want God Almighty to have the credit for giving me something up here beside a hat rack. God is the Architect. I am only His assistant."

"Preacher, baby," says Margaret, "why don't you sit down, so you won't be standing up over her." But he is almost deaf and likes to move around when he's listening to the inner word.

"We got to love each other before we can love God Almighty! I been preaching for sixty-one years. Any information you want to know about living, I am qualified by the Holy Spirit to give you the answer."

"I wish you'd sit down," says Margaret.

"I don't preach to no one race of people, because we are all God's children."

"That's right," says the chorus of Margaret and friend.

"In the heart we are the same."

"That's right."

"Thank God for you all. We are not far apart. We are not harming each other this morning. We not in the hospital. Isn't that a blessing? God wants us to love one another as He has loved US! Let the world know that you know THE MAN. I know The Man. Nothing can hurt me. You can kill my body, but there's a man on the inside, you can't kill!"

As I sit in the bus and listen, I think—let the hecklers give their seats up to poor old ladies. Let them stand at the rear and listen. "The Church has got to come together on one accord. All race of people got to get together. And see no black and no white. See no China, no Russia, no Germany, but All God's children, no denomination. Every race is welcome here!

"Don't ask God for no money. Don't ask Him for no home. Only, Sister, ask God for wisdom and knowledge, and you do the rest yourself. Even people that despise you, hate you, love them too. Love your family. Don't do the wrong thing. Let Jesus be your shepherd. Let Him be your doctor. Let Him be your lawyer. Let Him be shoe for your feet. Let Him be your guide. Every day, change the way you are living towards each other."

Let us *all* be gathered into Hermon's bouquet, filling the pews now, ready for the ride. There are plenty of seats for All Is Welcome—*GLORY Hallelujah!*

Our Lady of Blind River, the Madonna Chapel, and Noonie Smith's Memorial Chapel

Driving down the Old River Road in Ascension Parish, trying to find Tezcuco Plantation in the dark, we see a ghastly glow in the distance. Soon huge refinery plants appear in the fields on either side, towers spewing, blasting out a hellish light that illuminates the unearthly-looking structures. Hard to imagine any man inside those nighttime slave ships, but I'm sure there *are* men, working the night shift, possibly descendants of those who worked these same fields.

On waking, we encounter a different atmosphere. A foggy dew-drenched light comes through the massive live oaks that surround the old plantation. Wandering through formal walkways, over to the white, octagonal chapel, I find it an appealing shape, though on the inside, with its oversized saints, it has the feeling of a stage set. The original rustic log chapel, which the black population used for worship, burned down long ago.

After breakfast, we are off to meet Charlie Duhe at St. James Landing on Highway 61, halfway between New Orleans and Baton Rouge, close to the little town of Lutcher, in the heart of Cajun country. Charlie pulls up in his boat right on time, and we are ready to head down the bayou to find Martha DeRoche and *Our Lady of Blind River*.

It is wonderful to be out on the water, whizzing along in the cool morning air. Cypress trees, draped with lichen-green Spanish moss, are in abundance here. Martha and Bobby DeRoche are the only full-time residents on Blind River, and I am surprised at how far we have to go to reach their pier.

Finally we spot the cypress shingles of the little church, announcing itself in an all-American way, with flag and bell and barking dogs. Martha comes rushing out onto the dock in a bright red shirt, shouting, "Happy Valentine's Day!" Suddenly I am sorry I have not brought chocolates or a bunch of flowers.

The morning light is getting brighter, and Donna wants to shoot the exterior before we dock, so Charlie takes us up and down the river, back and forth, while Donna clicks away. In retrospect, I realize how it would have been nicer for me to get out, greet our hostess, and let Donna do her work, but that is hindsight. As we finally pull in to dock, Charlie mentions how there is a lot of bad blood between him and Martha. This becomes apparent as we get closer. She doesn't want to have anything to do with Charlie Duhe.

We try to reassure her as we enter the little cypress chapel, but our tentative, teasing arrival has aggravated her, and she breaks into tears of frustration. "I just can't take it no more, what the people are doing. They're looking for *vainglory,* and I'm not *looking* for vainglory. All I want is, what I do is the labor of Jesus and Mary and the Holy Spirit and the Father, and they have been so good, they have rewarded me so much."

A blue-robed Madonna with welcoming arms stands serenely above the altar in a huge hollowed-out cypress stump, which Charlie and his wife sculpted and varnished. Martha has draped the wooden grotto with a bright blue cloth to obscure the twelve-hundred-year-old log. Smaller cypress niches in the back corners, filled with Spanish moss, feature Joseph and Jesus. These little logs, each a bit smaller than the next, like Matrushka dolls, were taken from the inside of the large hollowed-out portion.

At one time, plagued by drink and depression, Martha was on medication and attempted suicide, but then she began to have visions and locutions, and convinced her husband that they should build *Our Lady of Blind River,* which she describes as the "Lourdes of the Bayou." Martha confided her dream to family friend Val Amato, and he gathered thirty-seven friends together, mostly hunters and fishermen and their wives, and everything was made by hand, including the 2,000 hand-hewn shingles, cypress planters, hand-painted donation box, silk flowers, and even the crocheted cloth beneath the bible.

"The love that built this chapel," Martha exclaims, "was a special miracle." There are three cypress pews on either side of the aisle, and the altar itself is encircled by cypress knees, a low fence of knobby protrusions, sculpted by the elements, and now preserved with coats of shellac. Construction of the chapel began on Easter Sunday 1983, and though the DeRoches have not received any official recognition by the Church, they had a dedication on August 21 of that same year. Boats lined the pier, and hundreds of local people gathered to celebrate.

Fifteen years later the chapel is still going strong, and many people have felt the benefit—"People without work, people with back trouble, people with leg trouble, any disease you can talk about, they've been receiving blessings, in all phases of life." There are volumes of visitors' names and addresses, people who have managed to make their way to *Our Lady of Blind River* from cities all over the world. That alone seems miraculous.

When people make donations, Martha uses the money to buy finger rosaries and brown cloth scapulars. She is afraid of the people who want to develop the river, because they are not putting God first. "I have put God first from the very beginning. We never wanted this to be a place where people could profit. I did open my mouth one time, because this woman brought some high-class people, well-to-do people, and she thought I was going to give the explanation of the tree altar, and not speak of God. They don't want the power of Christ on this river. I've seen people that come from tourism and made like they were putting money in the donation box, faking it. Don't come abuse this chapel for your profit and not put God first. If they put God first, they're going to come out ahead. But this tour lady said, 'You embarrass me,' and she walked out. 'You embarrass me in front of those people. You never did do this before. You never talked in praise like this before.' She really called me down."

Martha is impassioned about a photograph of Our Lady, who appeared outside the entrance to the chapel. The photograph was

taken by Jimmy Ordoyne with a one-step Polaroid camera. "When his picture developed, he looked up into the heavens. I said, 'Jimmy, what you got there, Darling?' I looked at it, and my first words were, '*Oh Jimmy,* The Blessed Mother's telling you something. Our Lady of Blind River's telling the world something! Praise God, praise Jesus and Mary.' I said, 'Look, look Jimmy, this can't happen! This is done by the hand of God.'"

Bobby DeRoche is inside their waterfront home before the TV. He has cancer and rheumatoid arthritis and needs a foot operation, but he's seen enough hospitals for one life, and refuses to undergo any more surgery. Martha has outdone herself and made us a real Cajun lunch with white beans, roux and sausage ladled over rice, salad with cucumber and tomatoes, Dr. Pepper. We are famished, and help ourselves to seconds while she talks:

"People think I'm naive. They think I don't know what's going on. One time I was talking about my visions, and this man was laughing at me in the chapel. I told him, 'You hearin' the truth, Darling. This is not a cult.' And he popped out laughing. So I told his wife, 'Is that your husband, Darling?' She said, 'Yes Ma'am,' and I said, 'Darling, you're going to have a miserable life.' She says, 'I'm already having one.' I said, 'I'm going to pray for you right now,' and I went outside and he was laughing and laughing. He had a cigarette in his hand. He was probably smoking dope. There have been people so drunk, they could hardly make it out of their boats and up the stairs. I tell you this river needs cleansing.

"They got a bar-room down on the river where they all go to gossip. I ask for perseverance and endurance every day. We go into the town of Grammercy now, they turn their backs, don't even tell us a hello anymore, because of the people's bad-mouth talking. They're saying I'm hallucinating. They're saying I'm doing all this on my own—we're doing it for the money— we're doing it because we want to be public. We *never* asked *anyone* to come here, not newspapers, not television, *no one,* and we've never asked anyone for any help except for Mr. Val Amato, the man who God sent to have this chapel built. I have been called a fanatic on religion. So here I am, a fanatic on religion. I didn't want to hurt anyone. I guess God allows people to be hurt in order for the truth to be known. I guess He knows *that* book. He knows it! He knows you got to be hurt in order for some good to come."

Returning to Lutcher that afternoon, we head over to White Castle. Grand plantation homes along the bends of the Mississippi River sit like big elegant cakes set out for a cake walk. Passing Nottaway Plantation and continuing on down Old River Road to Plaquemine, we find the sweetest cupcake of a chapel we've come upon. The *Madonna Chapel* is painted a fresh white, and has its own miniature spire and single gothic blue window set above its double front doors. According to the 1934 edition of Ripley's *Believe It or Not,* this is the "smallest church in the world," measuring nine feet square.

Originally built by a poor farmer, Anthony Gullo, in 1903, the chapel is now taken care of by Mitzie and Anthony Roppolo, who live a few houses down the road. Despite the fact that Mr. Roppolo has had two hip replacements recently and has not been able to do the work he would like to do, the lawn is cut and the grounds are beautifully maintained. The setting is particularly serene and sunny, and we are in need of a little serenity. As we walk down the cement stairs, flanked by evergreen trees, we pass into the yard of the chapel, held in by a tidy picket fence, with horses and cows grazing in a distant pasture.

When I close the chapel doors behind me, a subtle blue light comes through the window, illuminating a figure of Mary. I sit down in this tranquil, filtered light, alone for a moment, absorbing it.

At the turn of the century, when one of Anthony Gullo's children survived a critical illness, he ordered the central figure of the Madonna from Italy and proceeded to build this little chapel as a response of thanks. Plaquemine, Louisiana, was originally an Italian settlement, and the aesthetics here do seem European. Mitzie Roppolo remembers walking with her Italian grandmother down the gravel road as a child, gathering flowers along the way, and bringing their bouquets to the little chapel when they came here to pray their daily rosary. Growing up, Mitzie felt that the *Madonna Chapel* was very special. "It was nice to have such a holy place close to home. Ever since I was a child," Mitzie admits, "I've been close to the Blessed Mother. We are Eucharistic ministers in church. People who don't have faith—who don't pray—I don't know how they go through life."

There is a tradition of saying the rosary in the chapel every morning at 7 A.M. from August 1st to the 15th. The community is particularly proud that they still say Mass here once a year, on August 15th—the date of the Blessed Mother's Assumption into Heaven. On that day the neighborhood erects a canopy just outside the church. Over two hundred people usually attend the service, staying on for a cake sale and raffle, which help to raise money for chapel upkeep and improvement. You can tell that this place has been well loved and cared for—the floorboards and the inner siding are new, and everything seems freshly painted. The chapel was originally built in an octagonal shape, and though it has been restructured somewhat, the inner wall around the raised altar still reflects those angles, and the curves almost seems to embrace me as I rest in the calm blue light.

Mrs. Roppolo tells me that there have been magazine and camera crews out to photograph this exquisite little jewel, and once an interviewer asked her what was so special about the chapel, expecting that she would talk about the architecture of the place, its charming size, or perhaps the big bell set atop its own wooden tower out in the yard. But Mitzie responded, "What's special? The *Madonna Chapel* is dedicated to the Mother of God—what could be more special than that?"

I am sorry to leave this lovely place, but we decide to push on, down Highway 1 all the way to Golden Meadow near the Gulf of Mexico—it looks like the drive will take about two hours, which would get us to *Noonie Smith's Memorial Chapel* just before sunset. If we are to go, we have to go now.

We pass church after church with a packed parking lot, everyone inside for Saturday afternoon Mass. Thank God they are not out on this two-lane highway. The drive is taking us longer than expected. If we arrive after sunset, all our efforts will have been wasted, but as always on this trip, it seems that things work out. We pull up onto the gravel apron before the memorial chapel with ten minutes of light left in the sky.

Noonie Smith is a Cajun *maw maw*. Her black-trimmed, matchbox chapel is perched up on cinderblocks amidst tall pampas grass, alongside Bayou Laforche, with its shrimp boats and trawlers. But it is a sad sight—the two cement crosses on either side of the steps, for her two deceased sons, Livingston and Abraham.

Livingston died of encephalitis at three years old. The tragedy was so devastating to Mrs. Smith that she was checked into Charity Hospital in New Orleans, and received emotional support from understanding psychiatrists as well as from the priests and sisters there. Almost twenty years later tragedy struck again, and she lost her teenage son, Abraham. He died in her arms. "The kid who bagged my groceries that afternoon, stabbed my son later that evening."

I think any mother who has lost a child, not to mention two sons, must be an authority on prayer. No wonder so many people stop here, often fifty a day, and no wonder she sometimes assumes the role of confessor, or open-hearted listener to others who are suffering.

There is barely enough visibility to read the "Letters to God," that have been written on pink, yellow, and blue Post-its, stuck to the interior of the dark chapel walls. In the diminishing light, with wind blowing the pampas grass back and forth, the temperature seriously plummeting, I copy a few of these messages down:

> Dear God—Please pray for my family.
> I am on drugs. My son doesn't know
> either my husband. Lisa
>
> *
>
> This is in Praise of the Blessed Mother
> for Giving Me Another Teaching Job and a
> Good One. thank you. love E.C.J.
>
> *
>
> Dear Jesus, ples help Mom and Dad
> to get a logn ples
>
> *
>
> Please pray that my
> baby brother get to know
> his son some day again
> Thank you
> God Bless Us
>
> *
>
> Please Watch over my baby
> in Heaven. He was
> taken from me unwillingly
> in 1976. In loving memory of
> my lost

As the last of the late light sinks into the salt marsh, an egret flies over the chapel, heading east. Hurricane winds are predicted for tomorrow. As we head north out of Golden Meadow, we see the Evacuation Route signs all along the road. This is spirit country, but it is rough territory too. Noonie used to lock up the chapel after hours, but one night, a man so desperate to pray broke through the black double doors, and she realized then that a place of God should always be open. Sometimes people need God even more after sundown.

PRIESTESS MIRIAM

New Orleans, Louisiana # Erzulie's Altar

Priestess Miriam's exotic, feminine nature emanates from her like a fragrance from a flower. Dressed in fabulous African regalia, she speaks with a melodious, lulling voice while showing us around the storefront rooms of her spiritual temple. Every possible bit of wall space is decorated to the hilt, with multiple altars everywhere. There is so much to see one can hardly take it all in— a black Madonna holding a black baby Jesus, African sculptures, food offerings for ancestors, dolls, baubles, the head of a pink ceramic flamingo, bottles of whiskey and perfume set out for certain *loa,* or spirits. I am amazed at the assemblage of things—no Soho artist could improve on this—amazing, curious, peculiar, strange, but not dark and forbidding like some of the commercial voodoo shops you see near Bourbon Street. This looks like the accumulated work of a lifetime.

Miriam agrees. Before Christmas they did a little house cleaning, and removed the entire contents of the temple. "We thought, one week to paint and put back, but it took three weeks taking everything down. Now it's nice and clean and dainty." She laughs her infectious, musical laugh.

Admittedly, I first approached Priestess Miriam with some reservations. When Patsy Lowry, of the straw bale chapel, suggested I visit Miriam and her *Voodoo Spiritual Temple,* my first response was, "Oh no, I don't want that in my book." But my own reaction made me stop and wonder if this was merely the typical white folks' fear response to the powerful pulse of black culture. Some might say that fear of black magic is biblically justified, but I have noticed that very similar practices of ancestor worship common in Catholic

120

Latino cultures are viewed as relatively benign, non-threatening. I would venture to guess that our fear of voodoo springs in part from a deep guilt about our consistent mistreatment of the black population. It's amazing to think that our country, based on religious freedom, denied that freedom—indeed *all* freedom—to an entire race. No doubt there is fear of reprisal.

Despite the attempted religious repression of slaves, the African American population has always been a passionately spiritual people. When drumming was denied them, spirituals were born. I have always been attracted to the almost physical spirituality I have experienced in black gospel churches, from the *Soul Saving Station Across the Nation* in Saratoga Springs, where I went to college, to the Mother's Day Gospel Concert in Oakland, California, to our black gospel Catholic sister church in the Bronx, St. Augustine's. When their chorus enters in slow procession, I can feel the visceral, spine-tingling presence of the Holy Spirit, and I wonder why—Why is the Spirit called down into their midst in such a palpable way? Why is rhythm so ingrained in this version of reverence—rhythm and repetition, so necessary to any art? Why does prayer move through the physical body more naturally with black culture? Why are most white congregations stiff and still, reserved and self-conscious, while black congregations get to drum and call out when they worship? Who was the Lord of the Dance, after all?

121

As Miriam speaks, it is sometimes hard for me to follow—her words seem to ride on the waves, flowing out, further out, then washing back in again. She is in touch with a special intuitive knowledge. The unseen world of spirit is everywhere. She believes that the spirits continually influence our lives and that we have to make peace, to keep an ideal balance of harmony. Perhaps what people fear most about voodoo is its connection to this realm of spirit, which many feel is an area that should remain out of bounds, too dangerous for vulnerable human beings.

But Miriam laughs and loves with such a radiance I fear no malice here. Her presence is warm and sensual, soothing and calm. She seems more like a natural healer than a witch doctor, and indeed, she says, the images of voodoo conjured up by Hollywood have done more to warp impressions of black spirituality than anything else.

Erzulie's altar looks lovely. I wonder if she is the African equivalent of the Virgin, and Miriam explains—"Erzulie is that which God or the Sun comes face to face with every morning, and that's the beautiful part of it, because it takes Erzulie to generate the energy throughout the world. The overview and the underview. She is the other half of the coin. When we look at the elements, at the solar system, the sun and the moon, the order of day and night, what really balances the whole energy of that is the water. The water is the most feminine product of the universe. Without it, nothing moves. What we're looking at with Erzulie is the heart. On the physical level, we start with the ocean and go to the sea, go on to the gulf, to the lake or the river . . ."

"And then to the bathtub," I insert, and we laugh.

"When you look at the human structure, you look at the heart, and the blood goes on to the veins and the capillaries—same as the water on the face of the earth, pumping and rocking, like *Rockin' me Baby,* so when we rise up, we have the same energy, the same as the ocean. The earth keeping things balanced, and that keeps the breathing. As the sun rise up over the horizon and the heat penetrate the water, it send out that vapor—it stimulate and light up, and that's what the feminine does to the masculine. He comes forward, and he focus on her, and then if she in her glory, if all is well, she send out an illumination. We come together to carry on a higher endeavor of God in the universe. The Sun, the masculine, is the mirror that greets the feminine, and if the feminine decides she wants to shine with him she will, and if not, she send out a smoke of clouds—*Hey baby, I ain't shining today!*

"All things settle at Erzulie's feet. She is the highest energy in the world, because nothing can be productive without the stimulation of the mother. So mother has a great height in the universe. God claim just the masculineship, then nothing happens, but when He claim the two-folds of nature together, then He can be greatly productive."

Erzulie's *vévé* drawn in chalk on the floor is a ritual diagram of astral forces. Her *vévé* is an appealing design with a heart in the middle of complicated scrollwork. Erzulie seems to have kinship with the Greek goddess Aphrodite, connected with love and beauty, and all her toiletries—perfume, soap, lace, jewelry—but she also has a penchant for jealousy, vengeance, and discord—a very feminine figure!

Although voodoo is an earth-based religion, it is also a religion of the universe, in which the *loa* and ancestors are honored and revered. A great deal of voodoo prayer and practice is draped with the cloth of Catholicism. Perhaps this covering was the only way West African tradition could survive in the New World. As Miriam explains, "Voodoo in America exists under a different order. In America you have the Spiritual Churches, and the Spiritual Churches practice Christianity, but use the base of healing—lighting candles, giving potions, *bacas,* mojo bags, and helping peoples to work through difficulties that this work was designed to do. And so voodoo has survived under the Spiritual Churches. It would lean toward Catholic, because people will find that working with the saints you find more peace or serenity."

In voodoo the *loa* often relate to different saints in the Catholic Church. "Saint Anthony would be like Legba, Papa Legba, one aspect—opening the door, helping you to find your path. St. Thérèse is like Madam Bridget, understanding how to live in this side as well as to accept death, as a challenge to work from the celestial to the physical, as well as working from the physical to the celestial. She represents twenty-four. When St. Thérèse passed, she was at the age of twenty-four—it represents stability, which is the order of the day, of the time, completion."

But when Priestess Miriam talks about time, she might be talking about awakened time and the spirit of the universe—"We're coming into a time when celestial forces is more working than the human. It's time for the human to push back. Amazing that when the Pope left Cuba the flood came. It was such a good thing the Pope did down there. The falsehood of Castro—he couldn't deny the Holy Father from coming, but what were Castro's intentions underneath?"

I question her about the black magic aspect of voodoo, putting curses on people, and she responds, "Yesterday this lady comes in and she has this issue, and she feels that the issue is so bad with this person that she wants to make him paralyzed, and I said, 'You don't tell me what I can do.' I say, 'This person's energy is already causing you pain, so why do you want to come and tell me to cause more pain, that this pain will continue to exist? Better to get rid of the pain all the way around.' I say, 'You want the person to move forward away from you, then let's work in the order of spirit, not in the order of your say, or my say. And however spirit want this situation to be treated, then it will be treated for the best of each person.'"

Standing beneath Erzulie's altar, I am reminded of the holy-carnival collection acquired through the teen years of heightened romance, where every artifact takes on a kind of reverential aspect—Valentine candies hang alongside religious statues, palm fronds and lace, Erzulie's boat sailing on a sea of precious stuff, its mast stuffed with folded dollar bills that tourists have left behind for good luck in love.

I ask her about this image of the boat, and she says, "The image of the boat is very good in terms of carrying things. It's like the thought of God, the idea of Him. If I create me a vessel, I can *load it up* with all kinds of energy that can work forever, and so we're like that ship on water. Setting the stage for something greater, for life."

I see that she wants what we all want, that she hopes for a positive impulse that will build a united kingdom—she believes this is already happening throughout the world, and it is why I am here, talking to her now.

I agree, and yet still I have more questions. Why do they use the blood sacrifice of chickens and doves in voodoo ceremonies?

She says it's because of the energy. "In Chicago, I was doing an altar in the courtyard, and I was taken away in a trance—elevated. The physical body was lighting the charcoal and putting the incense on there, but I was taken away in this rapture. And I could see in the north so many cedars, and a cloud of smoke coming up through the cedars, and then all of a sudden this big sea of water was in front of me, and there was this white chicken on the water, on the edge.

"And then in a vision, I was up on this high hill, and I was dancing with this white chicken, and the heavens opened up—the whirlwind rose up out of the valley, and then this cage descended from on high, and it set on this pedestal and it opened up and out came two turtle doves. That was just before I met my husband."

Priest Oswan Chamani, born in Belize, Central America, was a gifted herbalist. He became Miriam's partner in this spiritual work at the *Angel Angel All Nations Spiritual Church* in Chicago. It was his idea to move to New Orleans, where they opened the temple in 1990. "But he passed several years ago," she says. "His birthday is coming up soon."

She takes me out back to the courtyard, where she's suddenly overwhelmed by the feeling that I've been here with her before. It does feel oddly familiar, but I assure her I've never been in this courtyard. She persists, positive that we sat here together and talked. "That's a trick on me this morning!" she laughs. Taking me back to the chicken coop, she shows me a beautiful big black rooster with several hens. "That's Mr. Rooster," she beams. "My husband told me before he passed that we needed a black rooster on the courtyard. He's like a spiritual messenger. Look—he jumped up there—he wants you to really see him."

"I see you!" I say. "You're beautiful, yes you are!"

"Are you gonna crow for Laura?" Miriam asks. "You going to say good morning?" He clucks and struts around the cage.

"When people come to the spiritual houses, they looking for a wider view of life. They're not looking to be placed on the same existence where they were brought up. If we leave them confused when they come to the spiritual houses, then where would they go? But you can't live in another state unless you have mastered the state you are in. And after that, then we all will fly away to the other side and begin a new existence."

Hale County, Alabama # A Chapel Made Out of Tires

After a five-hour drive from New Orleans, stopping along the way for a southern lunch of field peas, rice, collard greens, and cornbread, we pull into Eutaw about 2:00 P.M. and wend our way toward Yancy, a lovely rolling piece of property with a small home set above a natural pond, owned by two women, Lemuel Morrison and Retha Brannon, but only Ben, the black caretaker, is there, sweeping up.

Soon Ruard Veltman, one of the three young chapel builders, arrives from Montgomery, where he has a new job with McAlpine & Tankersley, a lively firm that deals mostly with upper-end residentials. Ruard is a tall, handsome twenty-seven-year-old with an unassuming, self-assured presence.

In January of 1995, he and Steve Durden and Tom Trethaway, all contemplating their thesis building project, joined forces and came up with the idea for a chapel. A local resident, Lemuel Morrison, was open to the idea. "When we looked over her property," Ruard says, "we stumbled upon this bluff. In this area you have rolling hills, but rarely anything like a fifty-foot drop. We all agreed on the site—that was the easiest part."

An original long cement cow trough, with metal stanchion, acts as a kind of entranceway, slanting down toward the site, a reminder that this was once a working dairy farm. I like the fact that this was where the cows came to feed—a nice metaphor for an entrance to a holy place, where one comes for spiritual food. The trough is also in harmony with the slightly dilapidated look of the chapel, for the roof, very consciously, was intended to suggest a caved-in barn structure. The element of collapse, which conveniently lets in southern light, only adds to the ultimate experience of the inside, which is surprisingly spacious.

I ask Ruard how they decided on using old tires for the chapel walls, and he says that came about during an Easter dinner. Ruard was talking with his father about the project and wondering what material they could use when another guest said, "Well out West they build out of tires." Everybody thought that was a great idea. Ruard's father works for Michelin, and so it was also a suitable homage.

"Tires are free. You're recycling, and all you need is manpower, and we had that." Ruard describes how they had to pound each tire full of dirt until it inflated and became rock hard. "Once the tire is laid in place it weighs two hundred to three hundred pounds, and you can't move it. We could get about

thirty tires done a day amongst the three of us. And we did a thousand tires—that's about thirty-three solid days of doing nothing but pounding dirt. I was in much better shape three years ago."

Though Ruard has a lot more to tell us about *Yancy Chapel,* he has also brought along plans to another chapel he's currently working on for Carolyn and Wynton Blount, an Old English timbered structure, which they commissioned for their property, Wynfield. While *Yancy Chapel* cost only about $8,000 to build, the Blounts' memorial chapel may cost as much as a hundred times more. In contrast to the reclaimed quality of *Yancy Chapel,* only the best possible materials are being used by the Blounts—fieldstone, limestone, and quarry stone will compose the two-foot-thick walls. "The whole chapel sits down into the earth, so that the windows are almost at ground level," Ruard explains, as he unrolls the plans. "You will be able to sit by the window, reach out, and feel the grass."

Ruard seems slightly apologetic, having moved so quickly from the struggling, socially conscious Rural Studio program into the luxuries of the estate set, from salvaged tires, tin, and timber to one-inch-thick pieces of roofing slate, wrought ironwork made in Germany, and hand-blown leaded glass. Though every detail in this new chapel will be a considerable work of art, the ultimate look will be somewhat simple. The interior dimensions are only 11 × 22, similar to the size of *Yancy Chapel.* I particularly like the treatment of one exterior wall that falls into ruins like a folly, with a nice crumbling effect.

Ruard, who is the project architect on this job under the direction of Bobby McAlpine, tells me that when he first presented the design to the Blounts, it was all hand drawn on a long piece of linen. Certainly there is an element of the romantic here, but it seems that Ruard's heart and spirit are still back with Rural Studio, one of the most innovative architectural projects in the country, sometimes jokingly referred to as *Taliesen, Deep South.*

At the Rural Studio, architecture students from Auburn University have an opportunity to come to an isolated area where they design and build structures for the community, most often experimental homes for members of the poor black population. Over dinner, program director Samuel "Sambo" Mockbee explains that they try to incorporate social and political values as well as aesthetic ones. "I make sure we deliver a piece of architecture," he says. *Yancy Chapel* is certainly that, for the Whitney Museum of New York has listed it as one of the two hundred most interesting twentieth-century architectural sites in America.

It is raining like mad outside right now as we sit around a huge dining-room table in the on-loan antebellum mansion where Rural Studio is presently housed. "They had great weather that whole winter," Mockbee remembers of the *Yancy Chapel* project. "They'd be pounding with their shirts off, and they'd come in at night and be all hot and nasty—we'd call it pounding naked. And one day I took this sixty-five-year-old retired teacher out there— she wanted to see the chapel construction, and I was telling her—Now look, they do what we call pounding naked, and we might drive up on it. I honked the horn, and nobody stirred or nothing, so I thought maybe they'd gone to eat lunch. The tires were only about so high off the ground, just old tires and dirt. So we started walking out toward the chapel, and Ruard must have been taking a cat nap, lying down there behind the tires, because when he heard us, he raised up, and from here on up he *was* naked. Broad-chested and manly and everything, and she went— *Oh My God! Isn't he beautiful!* But he had his shorts on. He wasn't total."

You can see that Sambo Mockbee has a lot of fun teasing his students. You couldn't be thin-skinned and last around here. Sambo is a busy man, gruff and witty, a great teacher who gets results because of his high expectations. It is clear that he is proud of Ruard, but he would rather not say so directly.

Sambo seems to like the fact that these boys made such an inspired piece of architecture for so little money. Salvaged tin was taken from an old barn and cut into shingle-size pieces that accommodate the parabolic twist of the roof line. "The tin is not terribly permanent," Ruard admits, "but there's something beautiful about an old rusted roof. The rafters are all hard pine beams taken from a house that Retha and Lemuel gave us. The rafters play a big part in the motion—it makes the building feel like it's about to take off. The ridge

Photo by Jon Tate

beam," he says, "is very heavy, but it almost appears to be floating.

"During construction people would come out and help us. One day we were piecing the ridge beam together—we built it on the flat cement ground of the trough, as we needed to make it very accurate. We made a platform on top of the scaffolding, and we had to get this ridge beam on top. I thought we'd have to take it all apart, and put it back together, but then a group of fourth-year students from Auburn stopped by to take a look at what we were doing, and we got them to help us. There were forty-five people picking up this eighty-five-foot-long ridge beam—the thing weighed a ton. It was kind of like a barn raising. After we got it in place, we had a huge fish fry with beer and music. It was terrific."

Returning to the site on the following morning, I notice that the use of water in the chapel is particularly appealing. The source is a natural artesian well in the upper pasture, and the water flows downhill at a gradual pace, spilling through a slit in the back wall that Ruard calls "the Angelic Grotto." The trickling water runs over a big sculptural piece of slate down into a trough—you have to step over it as you enter, though a metal grille keeps your feet from getting wet—then it continues to flow down along the left side of the chapel, down toward the pulpit, dropping into the wetlands below. The flow of the water represents life's journey, a metaphor for the continuous movement of life. As you look out at the natural expanse, the sound of the water is meditative, calming.

"Compression and release are important elements in this space," Ruard explains. "The walls are wider in the back—slanted out—and the roof is lower there. The whole idea is to move you through—to get you to this point where you are in nature—you feel surrounded by nature—you travel through this man-made structure and you go down into fellowship. You have descended, but you are still elevated above the wetlands beyond." At the open end of the chapel there is a walkway that moves you right out into the trees, which make a natural canopy. The pulpit, influenced by the Italian architect Carlo Scarpa, is a delicate combination of metal and concrete. With its three steps up, it also has a floating effect.

Ruard says that the three members of their design/construction team did not know each other well when the project began, but they developed quite a relationship through the grueling process of building. "We lived together. We drank together. We ate together. We built together. We practically slept together," he laughs. "There were times when we did not want to speak to each other, but by the end it was like brotherly love—that's what it felt like."

The chapel was completed just in time for Steve and Laura Durdin's September wedding. Though the parents of the bride questioned whether this was an appropriate place for their daughter to get married, it ended up being a joyful event with over three hundred people in attendance. Tiny white lights were strung on the long lane of hackberry trees that line the cement trough walkway, and big bouquets of flowers were placed on round metal dishes set at intervals along the stanchion.

This same dish shape is happily repeated inside at the font, extending from a tall found piece of metal that blocks one's view as you enter. I can imagine the bride pausing here, the groom still out of sight. The chapel can hold only about sixty people, so the other wedding guests crowded around the curves of the upper level under the roof line, where they actually had a better view of the service.

"We each had our own personal spiritual reaction to what we were doing," Ruard says. "I'm at that age when I question my faith. I was raised Catholic, and I still am, though I didn't let that play a big part in this. I was more concerned about what does it take to build a spiritual space? What do you do? Usually people come in here and they don't speak. But Steve was about to marry into Catholicism and he was learning all there was to know, and he would question me about everything. Steve was more about meaning, while Tom was this ramjet—*Let's get it done!* And I'd have to say, No, we have to think about this. What was great about this project was that each of us was very different. We all loved to build. We all loved to be out-of-doors. If we had three people like me, it never would have gotten made. This was a great balance."

Little Rose Chapel Continues

Oh happy day! My gardening friend Georgene calls to talk about her baby shower and the upcoming labor, but I can tell she has something more to say, one little request. She is hesitant as she asks, "You know, Dave and I want to get married before the baby is born, and we were wondering how you'd feel about our using the chapel?"

I am delighted. Of course, of course! It's as if a preemie were on the way, wanting to be born before we're even ready. But we are thrilled and grateful to receive. Our first event in Little Rose Chapel.

We don't have an altar, but we can carry out a table and cover it with a cloth. The chapel doesn't have any heat, but we can borrow a space heater. Georgene will bring big bouquets of anemones, and we'll provide the champagne to celebrate afterwards. Little Rose Chapel is underway!

It hasn't all been easy building this chapel, but I'm sure we will forget the difficulties, as one forgets the pain of childbirth. Whenever money is being spent, there is always anxiety, but as Lori Mendez once said, "Don't worry about the expense—It will be worth it!"

It is a particularly wonderful surprise when a beautiful hand-carved statue of St. Thérèse arrives from Santa Fe, made by Manuel Gurule, another gifted santero. Manny has taken such exceptional care with every possible detail, from the lovely opening folds of her robe to the carving of her expressive hands. Even the little scraffito marks scratched onto the hand-painted surface make for a special decorative touch. Beneath the base are these words: Hecho con mucho cariño para Laura Chester especialemente, Manuel Gurule, 1998. *(Made with much loving care.)*

When I call to thank him, I can't praise him enough. I ask about the wonderful colors he used, and he says that he first covered the statue with a hand-made gesso made from animal resin glue. This rawhide-like material is melted down with water, and then plaster gypsum is added. An application of this substance makes the jelutong wood impermeable. Though cottonwood roots were traditionally used in making bultos, many of the santeros are now using this fine-grained wood that yields so easily to carving.

He says that a group of santeros recently went out on a search party together, taking along food and drink to share as they looked for earth colors they could use in their painting. In the little town of Regina, New Mexico, they found rock that contained the warm golden ochre Manny used for St. Thérèse's robe. The stone has to be pulverized and mixed with water to make the paint. The blue indigo that covers the base of the statue was made with a dark inky powder mixed with gum arabic, while the black of her hood was a mixture of indigo and walnut. Finally, to protect her, Manny made a varnish of piñon pitch and Everclear alcohol, and then waxed her with natural beeswax. When she came out of the box, arms overflowing with tiny satin roses, she smelled of honey. I had to kiss her hello.

You can tell that Manny must have fallen in love as he was working on his St. Thérèse—so much time and care went into her creation. He tells me he is now working on a retablo of her, which will be Donna's gift to Little Rose Chapel. How blessed we are by all the people we have met on this Holy Personal pilgrimage. Manny's wife, Sophia, is exceptionally warm and lovely, and a good correspondent. I feel we have made very dear, long-lasting friends.

But not everything in the building of our chapel has gone easily. I have trampled upon a few male egos, and have not been as kind as I might have been, worrying over bills and wanting my way. After several missed appointments and unanswered phone calls from a mason friend, we decide to do the interior stucco work ourselves.

Mason and Peter Shepley have painstakingly created a barrel vault, which becomes a four-sided domed vault in the deeper half of the chapel. Hammering strips of wood and covering it with metal lathe, they slop on the deeply humid, chalk-smelling compound until the interior blossoms into this beautiful white *shape, curve upon curve—most astounding, how grand it seems all of a sudden though the interior dimensions are only 8 × 13 feet.*

We discover that the pink marble statue from Torcello is an exact replica of the Madonna from the apse mosaic in the Torcello cathedral, Santa Maria dell'Assunta. As the plaster goes up, the statue is embedded into the rear wall. I had wanted to put a circle of mother-of-pearl buttons and shells around her, but the plaster dries quickly and the opportunity passes. In any case, I'm changing my mind about the décor as things unfold, for the aesthetics seem to want to remain fairly clean, rather than funky. Despite Mason's protests, I decide to put a spray of gilded wooden stars on the central arch—it's like walking beneath the Milky Way.

Mason comes up with a plan to put three niches as well as a small cupboard on either side of the front section. Pete wants to donate the cupboards as his gift, a gesture we appreciate. He and Mason have worked harder than anyone, almost on top of each other, slopping bucket after bucket of stucco up, as the space heater blasts away, and the walls perspire with this earthy odor. We have to keep the room above freezing. If the walls were to freeze now, the setting stucco could crumble.

The shape of the dome is perfect, and the acoustics are magical. We all agree that we want to outline the curves of the dome with gilded strips, which will meet where the Venetian-like lantern hangs with its single round beeswax candle. The shape of the rusty lantern makes a wonderful hexagonal design on the ceiling. Afternoon light pours in through the stained-glass windows, streaming through the cut glass flower shape, throwing a spray of pink and green droplets onto the altar.

Finally we are ready to clean. I tear down the plastic that covers the posts, the niches and font, pull out the plywood floor covering, and sweep the marble floor. A lot of stucco has puddled and hardened around the edges, but Mason chips it out, and I vacuum it up. I buy roses for the niches and fresh beeswax candles. To celebrate, Georgene and Dave, Barbara and Pedro come over for dinner. Pedro has brought a huge sea bass, but first Dave presents a fabulous baked brie with a pastry ribbon on top. What a feast!

After dinner we all go out to the chapel, walking over the crusty snow in the dark quiet. It is not a fiercely cold evening, but a nice winter feeling is in the air. The chapel holds us perfectly. With all the candles lit, the gilded cross in the center niche, it does seem like a holy place. I wish we could all burst into spontaneous song together, but Barbara is the only one among us expansive enough for that. I had worried about how Barbara would feel with Georgene so pregnant—Bar-

bara and Pedro have been undergoing the long arduous process of adoption. But everyone seems to get along in a most harmonious way. As we walk back out into the crisp cold beneath the stars, it feels like a blessed evening.

Perhaps because of its importance, the most difficult aspect of the chapel has been the creation of the altar. First there was the generous offer from Jim Fitzgerald, who said we could use old raw hunks of marble left out in his field. I collected a load with Jeff Albert, the mason who constructed the exterior walls of the chapel. I loved the natural, weathered surfaces of the field marble, but in an effort to shape the stone, Jeff torched them, and we ended up with a bright white look that was alarmingly clean.

My other mason friend thought I should look at a pallet of quartzite he had in his shop. I liked the creamy warmth of the stone with its irregular surfaces, and gave him the go-ahead, but when I dropped by a week later, I saw that he had begun laying out very small, brick-sized pieces of quartzite in a vertical rather than a horizontal pattern. I took an immediate dislike to it. The choppy verticality worried my eye. I wanted the altar to be elegant but not visually demanding. I wanted to trust him, as I appreciated his talents, but he didn't want to compromise, insisting that the stone should be laid out this way, that chapels were all about verticality. That seemed like a very male idea to me, for this feminine chapel was more about circularity, a feeling of embracing, roundness, warmth, and beauty.

Perhaps the best patrons give their artisans free rein, but I am not so lenient. Frustrated by the situation, we decide to build the altar out of wood. With the marble floor and stucco walls, it will lend a warming presence. We have a week now before Georgene and Dave's wedding, and Mason is out in his shop working away, bending and clamping the plywood to make a curved shape. Together Pete and Mason carry the unfinished altar out over sheer ice that has frozen like an undulating skating rink over the entire field, making the approach highly treacherous.

I worry about Georgene, being so pregnant. How will she ever get out to the chapel? But on the morning before the ceremony, we discover a new use for ski poles, as Georgene and I go out to examine the space. I have left the propane heater running, and the gas has used up so much oxygen that it is difficult to light the candles—the matches keep going out. We have to open the door to let in fresh cold air. Georgene has got to breathe! I drape the makeshift altar with a linen cloth and a piece of lace, while Georgene places bouquets of anemones all around. There is the sweet smell of beeswax and rose incense. Anne's two gilded French candleholders stand upon the altar with their golden lilies and sheaves of wheat.

That afternoon around four, Georgene and Dave and the justice of the peace arrive together, and again we carefully make our way across the frozen tundra. Georgene looks like a fairytale princess, beautiful in her golden velour dress, her long blonde hair flowing down her back. Standing together, they both have to suppress giggles of nervousness as they say their vows and kiss. I throw rose petals on them for a final blessing, and then we creep back to the house for cheese sticks and champagne as the sun sets behind the ridge, a glorious display.

Then we're off to dinner at Aubergine, just the four of us. As we are about to sit down, I see our friends Barbara and Pedro dining with another group. Barbara has photographs in hand—pictures of the little Russian boy they have been promised for adoption—Ivan Pavel—they will call him "Vanya." After years of anticipation the dream is finally coming true. Somehow this seems the perfect note to hear on this day of fulfillment.

Ten days later, a beautiful newborn arrives in the world, and soon a birth announcement follows: Ella Grace would like to announce that her parents finally got formally married (after a seventeen-year engagement) at Little Rose Chapel in Alford.

PART FOUR

Broken Open, Far West

Whosoever builds for God a place of worship, be it only as the nest of a grouse, Allah builds for him a house in paradise.

—Mohammed

Wine Cask Chapel

(previous page)
Mother Goddess Altar

Ziggurat, Crestone

Buddha, Crestone
Tibetan Altar, Manitou
Kachina, Flaming Stupa

(opposite) Moonlodge

Little Rose Chapel Dedication

DUNSTAN MORRISSEY

A Wine Cask Chapel Sonoma, California

A haven of roses, herbs, and careful plantings is set against a sweep of fields. The winter grass is brilliant, strewn with lupine and golden poppies. A gushing stream spills through a gulch, while a woodpecker pounds a tree. Still, a sense of silence envelops one. Storm clouds build, but they make the light even more spectacular—we have arrived at Sky Farm.

In this Benedictine hermitage, guests stay on retreat for a day to a month, making donations when possible. The two cabins, like the chapel, were made from large wine casks, each twelve feet in diameter. The cabins, simply furnished with futon and lamp, still retain a musky scent of the grape. Guests bring their own food and bedding, and are asked to refrain from talking and making eye contact, disposing themselves to the inner silence of the Word.

When Dunstan greets us, I am glad that we are allowed eye contact, for he has the most lively, loving blue eyes. Though seventy-four, he feels like a contemporary. When I question him about a hermit giving an interview, he only smiles and says that exceptions can be made. He goes on to explain that refraining from eye contact is not some kind of a hang-up. "On the contrary, it's therapeutic." For people who really want to go into silence, it's refraining from a dialogue of the eyes as well. "The word *monk*," he continues, "comes from the Greek word *monochos,* one who lives in solitude, but also—one who is One with everything and everyone. That is the essence of being a hermit. Opposites are meant to be reconciled. Being a hermit doesn't mean that you don't like people," he smiles again with his eyes.

139

Though Dunstan Morrissey doesn't live within a monastic community now, he has been a monk for nearly fifty years. In the tradition of the hospitable Benedictines, he offers us tea. "But be careful," he warns us about his Irish wolfhound, Sophie, "she's been known to run off with the cookies!" We settle down on the sofa in the late afternoon light, and he speaks with frequent, thoughtful pauses about his early years.

Converting to Catholicism in his senior year at Notre Dame, he knew he wanted to be a monk, but he was advised to wait. He went into the Foreign Service, the youngest vice consul at the time, and was assigned to Alexandria, Egypt, but despite this promising career, he eventually yielded to the greater calling.

After years in an Illinois cloister, Father Dunstan was given permission to leave for the island of Martinique, where he would be under the spiritual direction of Jacques Winandy, a retired French abbot and renowned biblical scholar. "I lived on Mont Pelée, you know, the volcano that erupted earlier in the century. The abbot lived at the top of the volcano, and I lived about half way down. I saw him once a week. After four years, I only saw him once every six weeks. He was the only person I saw all year."

There was plenty of food for Dunstan to eat growing right outside his lean-to—bananas, tubers, oranges. A few other necessities like rice, kerosene, and wine for the Mass were brought to Father Jacques, and then passed along to him. "It was a life outside of time," he recalls. "The very atmosphere was centering."

Dunstan goes on to say, "Observing silence one faces the unconscious." He pauses for a moment. "The unconscious is pacified through normal social intercourse. When that's cut off, then it gives you a kind of confrontation, which can be quite harrowing. In silence, the field of experience is greatly enlarged. You cannot compare the intervals that take place with normal experience. All I can say is that it was the most satisfying part of my life. I felt like I was a camel who stocked up with water during those few years. I do feel it is still with me, some residue is there."

Now that Dunstan lives in Sonoma, California, it is hard for him to say whether he lives in the world or in solitude, but it is clear that solitude is still fundamental to his existence. "I couldn't tell you how things happened, how I arrived here—extraordinary circumstances." For instance, he was given a hundred and twenty acres of unspoiled land by a mere acquaintance. This gift came as quite a surprise, for Pop Norrbom was very close with his money, and not even a Catholic. Eventually sixty of the lower acres were sold so that

Dunstan could afford to build his home, the Simone Weil Refectory, as well as the two guest cabins and chapel.

In a voice filled with reverence he tells me that the chapel is dedicated to the Son of Man. "For me that title goes to the heart of it. And it was never picked up on." When I ask him why he wanted to have his own chapel, his answer comes quickly—"Because the Eucharist is the center of things, you know. When I was in solitude, I would say Mass alone. But I never felt I was alone. The Mass is a *cosmic event*. A friend of mine is making a silver dove that will hang above the altar, which will house the sacrament." Dunstan is disappointed that it is not ready for us to see. People often come to the requiem Mass that he offers in Latin, but he also goes into the town of Sonoma on Sundays to receive the Eucharist, because he doesn't want to lose contact with the community. "All the things you can say about living in solitude have also to be negated."

Opening the double doors to the chapel, I see a swirling smear of red, a single pane of stained glass behind the altar. A friend, who was going to make a stained-glass window, went to Berkeley with him to get the materials—"They have these great showrooms, but when we saw that—good Heavens, why should you try to concoct a window when you have that? It's the blood of Christ, but also the Holy Spirit. In the mornings, the floor is dappled with it."

We light the candles in the oil-lamp chandelier, illuminating the dark curved walls. There is something wonderful about being embraced by this dark, cylindrical space.

Dunstan goes on to say that there was an unfortunate incident with the bishop when he inherited Sky Farm. The bishop wanted the property turned over to the diocese, but it's a tradition that monastic property is never in the hands of a bishop. Monasticism exists at the outer edges of the formal church structure, and hermetical life exists at the outer edges of monasticism, but the bishop was insistent. "He said that if Sky Farm was not turned over to the diocese, I would lose my canonical tie as a priest. I had to decide between a vocation as a monk and my vocation as a priest. I decided that I didn't need anyone's permission to be a monk, so I told him that, and was then deprived of the authority to exercise the duties of the priesthood. I can't perform marriage ceremonies, for example. That is unfortunate. But I can still do Mass here. No one can prevent me from that."

Dunstan would like Sky Farm to offer the possibility of a venture into the unknown, waiting at the edge of the unknown, waiting without expectation. "I think if one could speak of the spirit of Sky Farm, it's a good place for the practice of waiting. People will be happy here who cherish waiting as sustained attention. It has to do with the sense that to wait is to be alive.

"You know we had a fire here a year ago—it swept all through here. But our buildings were saved. It was a miracle. The fire came right up to the deck, and went around. These green fields were entirely black. There was an Episcopal minister staying here then, who apparently began his prayers with Carl Jung's active imagination. He was in the chapel, and I guess the red window started his active imagination—he said the Lord appeared to him in flames— He had a great basket and was pouring flames out of the basket—that's the way the image came to him. The next day the whole horizon was lit up with fire.

"I came into the house to pray, and on the wall in the dining room there is an icon of Elijah, the prophet Elijah—he is considered the patron saint against fire. When I pray I don't usually have images—but this was such an instructive event for me, because I must say there was an image of Elijah, and there wasn't an image. Both things were true. I was there for an hour. When I came out, I met the fellow outside, and he said, 'You'd better gather your valuables,' and I said, 'I have no valuables.' But then I thought of the painting of the Theotokos," which represents Mary as Mother of God. "I took that down, and then I went to take the painting of Elijah off the wall, and it wouldn't come off the wall. Of course it shouldn't come off. It was meant to stay. It is amazing. And the mind resists acknowledging it. Even now, I have resistance.

"Honestly, you know we are living in very critical times. People say that in any evolutionary shift, you don't know what the direction is going to be, but there are certain signs that a shift is taking place, and I think we are living in such times, whether it's the truth of evolution, or the end of the world or what, I don't know, but we are living in critical times, and these things just keep you alert, you know. Also vigilant."

The ceiling of the round, wooden chapel is conical, covered with straw tatami mats, while the walls are decorated with a collection of Russian icons. The mood is dark, interior, Byzantine. Dunstan points out one icon in particular that pictures the face of Christ. It was done by his good friend Prasanna, an East Indian Hindu. "For months he felt something coming on, and he would just sit before the canvas, and then one day he made this, and in four hours it was finished. He said he couldn't paint for six months afterwards, and he didn't care if he ever painted again. It's a *powerful* thing." Father Dunstan goes on to say that it is very clear in the gospel of John that death and resurrection are one mystery. We separate them liturgically in order to appreciate them, but it is one mystery, and here in this painting, it is also clearly one mystery.

I tell him about the experience I had in the *Basilica San Marco*, how I felt overcome by the Holy Spirit. He responds by

telling me that something very similar happened to Simone Weil in Assisi, how she felt compelled to kneel. "She couldn't do anything but kneel. And later when she was with her parents in Portugal, and they were having the blessing of the fleet—she had this great sense of solidarity with *everybody*— and she saw that Christianity was a religion of slaves. And then again, at a Benedictine monastery outside of Paris, she was there for Holy Week, and had this terrible migraine headache, and the Lord descended on her and took her— something that the mind could not construct. Here she was this raging, French, Jewish intellectual—she knew what she was talking about. André Gide, T. S. Eliot, and Camus spoke of her as the greatest spiritual genius of the twentieth century, though she always reckoned herself as an outsider. She once said she wished to be the color of certain unnoticeable insects. Now today, she would understand that to be a Christian makes you an outsider. I was branded by Simone Weil," Dunstan says, "but Edith Stein was the saint." It seems curious that he brings up Edith Stein, for even though I know little about her, I just purchased her autobiography, *Life in a Jewish Family,* to give to my goddaughter, Joanna.

Dunstan speaks about Edith Stein's remarkable life—she was a brilliant student and phenomenologist, but when she read the biography of St. Teresa of Avila, her life was completely transformed. Despite protestations from her devout mother, Edith became a Carmelite nun. During the war years she was sent to Holland, and every month she had to go off to Nazi headquarters to be registered as a Jew. When she went before the commander she was supposed to say *Heil Hitler,* but Dunstan thinks that she probably said something like *Praised be Jesus Christ.* Then one day, the Nazis came and gave her and her sister ten minutes to pack up. "She always had that deep sense of identity as a Jew. She knew, she understood that her people were going to be in for this. Those who survived Auschwitz said that she had this wonderful equanimity. She was so centered in the presence of the Lord."

One wonders how this Benedictine hermit came to have such a special connection with these two Jewish, intellectual, European women. It's almost as if they sought him out, and wanted to befriend him, teach him in secret. Is this what's behind having a personal saint?

Just before departing for Alexandria years ago, Dunstan went into a secondhand-book shop, and quickly took a book off the shelf. "My hand shook," he recalls. "It was Simone Weil. I bought it, went down the street to a restaurant. Perceptually everything was clear, the red and white checkered tablecloth, the wood paneling, the metal coffee urn. I read maybe two or three pages, and it was so powerful, I remember thinking—*This is the truth. I'll have to follow it or my life will be meaningless.*"

About ten years ago, the definitive biography of Simone Weil came out, and toward the end, the author gives an account of when Simone's books were published. Dunstan realized that in December of 1945 that book could not have existed, in the usual way that things exist. "I went to the Simone Weil Conference in Los Angeles and there were authorities there from Toronto and London and I asked around if it were possible that this book could have been available to me in December of 1945, and they said no, not possible. It alerted me to the fact that the contours of things are not as definitive as our perceptions."

The refectory at Sky Farm is dedicated to Simone Weil. Two ceramic guard dogs stand on either side of the steep steps as if it were the entrance to a Tibetan temple. Inside, on the ceiling, there is a painting of a dragon. I ask Dunstan if he has been influenced by Eastern traditions, and yes, he studied Zen in San Francisco, spent years in Bombay, as well as in a Himalayan Buddhist kingdom near Tibet. He even worked in a Cambodian refugee camp in Thailand. But he responds, "I make a distinction between syncretism and eclecticism. Syncretism in my mind always begins with great insecurity and greed. It thinks—Well, I have a Mercedes-Benz, I think I'll have a little Catholic communion too, maybe some yoga, that sort of thing. St. Paul says—*All things are yours. You are Christ's and Christ is God's.* That's what I call eclecticism. There's a *vast* difference. Superficially they seem the same, and people can be misled."

Since it is not practical for everyone to live in a hermitage, he believes that those who are living in solitude are somehow doing so for everyone. "It came to me about the second year when I was living in very restricted solitude that, somehow, I was being used in that way. However, I don't want to make a case for it, you know. I prefer to leave the idea on the back burner somewhere, so I don't get into any heroics about my life."

When it is time to leave, I feel the impulse to give Dunstan a hug, for I feel we have formed a real friendship in these few short hours, but he has a certain respectful reserve, and puts his hands together and bows slightly like a Buddhist monk. As we drive away, I think of him saying, "After all these years, sound or noise or conversation cannot compromise the silence." I imagine it is this same golden silence that lovingly holds the world.

JAMES HUBBELL

Mendocino, California Sea Ranch Chapel

Driving up Highway 1 along the coast of California, we are on the edge of the continent—earth and air meet the great Pacific. It is an arduous road, curving and dipping through pockets of fog and pine. The sky is grey, but the sun breaks through and lights up a dazzling patch of water. Shouldn't every day be proclaimed a holy day?

Sea Ranch, just south of Gualala, is a tasteful development of spare, weathered homes, so discreet you can almost drive by without noticing the ram's horn insignia that marks this private community. In contrast to the minimal lines of the modern homes, *Sea Ranch Chapel,* cradled in its undulating stone wall base, looks like a living organism. The swooping roof of cedar shingles reminds one of waves or ruffled feathers, a baby bird yearning to try out its wings.

When James Hubbell was hired by Robert and Betty Buffum to create a memorial chapel in honor of the son of good friends, Jim came up from his home in Southern California, and stayed with the bereft family for several days. He not only walked the land, but also studied their son's sensitive watercolors and etchings, which ultimately influenced the design of this unique wayside chapel. "Kirk's tender rendering of feathers, shells and bones were images that would not leave me," Jim says. "They seemed so much a part of this windswept coast."

Kirk, who died at the age of thirty-seven, was an aviator and passionate ornithologist, who believed that art was the intermediary terrain between the

146

world of nature and spirit. This little chapel brings those two worlds together. The wild, colliding planes of the roof line make me think of an exploding milkweed pod, with a spray of seed jettisoned from the peak in a sculptural gesture—tossed to the wind.

As I speak with Kirk's mother, it is clear that the life of her son lives on through family and friends and that the life of the chapel touches everyone who passes. Paging through the chapel scrapbook, I notice one entry in particular: *I give thanks for the life of the young man who died so that this chapel could be born.* Though her son died fifteen years ago, Kirk's mother is still visibly shaken when she speaks of him. Having three other children does not lessen the pain.

"I'm sure it's not anything you ever get over. He was so remarkable, such a loving son." Kirk's mother remembers how important it was for her to take part in making one of the mosaic patterns that spreads like a sunburst on the chapel floor. Together with various members of the Buffum and Hubbell families, she and her husband placed stones in the design, adding their personal marks as an offering.

The chapel remains open during daylight hours, and travelers often leave notes:

> On a solo bicycle tour from Portland, Oregon to San Diego, California, caught sight of the chapel out of the corner of my eye, and I was compelled to stop and turn around. Based on its shape alone, I had no idea of what it was. I was blessed to have it completely to myself for about twenty minutes. I lay with my back against the cool flagstone floor, watching the light through the stained glass. I will never forget these few moments of peace and reverie. Thank you.

*

> Dude! Saw the old chapel this last spring break and Wow, what a cool little thing you got there. I totally dug what you were promoting there. Keep up the awesome job.

*

> The most beautiful and peaceful work of love ever! (written on the back of a Parducci Cabernet Sauvignon label)

Hubbell tells me that he found an eagle feather and the bone of a deer right where the chapel now stands. "When I was a kid," he continues, "I really didn't understand adults very well, but I felt at home with nature. It has been the major influence on my work."

Today, as a mature artisan and architect, Hubbell adds, "I see myself first of all as a human being, and probably second as someone who is in love with life. And next as a sculptor. I think my talent is that I can work with a great many things and can cross over lines that are usually not crossed over."

Hubbell doesn't limit himself to any one medium. In 1985 he received the Special Award for Excellence in Craftsmanship from the California Council of the American Institute of Architects for his work in design, sculpture, wood, glass, stone, and metal. "I've never understood matter and spirit as being separate, and in the same way, I believe that various materials can be on friendly terms with each other. I don't think of a building with the absolute sense that at some pristine point it is finished. To me it's much more of an organic structure, something that has its own life, that continues on after it has been built."

One of Hubbell's most successful media is stained glass. "When I was quite young, I saw Notre Dame in Paris, and it got me interested in stained glass—the way the sun came in and filled the whole structure with this marvelous light—it's so different from painting and sculpture—it's more like music that actually wraps around you." In the *Sea Ranch Chapel* there are three very different stained-glass windows—one incorporated in the entrance doors reflects the forest behind; another rises like a tall, vertical wave; while the third rounded window is a swirl of color, reminiscent of a tide-pool. Looking through this colorful porthole, one can gaze all the way out to the sea.

Though many different craftsmen participated in this unique chapel, one primarily senses Hubbell's touch—even the comfortable teakwood benches are sculpted according to his direction. The central chandelier, the wrought iron grille before the *prie-dieu,* the needlepoint design on the kneeler were all Hubbell designs. The blossoming plaster ceiling, like angel wings exploding, was a grand part of his vision. Other more whimsical touches are noticed only by accident—little treasures of stone and abalone tucked into the walls here and there.

Hubbell's cosmic sensibility and approach to building is very much aligned with the spiritually based structures of Rudolf Steiner, as well as the organic buildings of the well-known Spanish architect Antonio Gaudi. But Hubbell's art is not just relegated to commissioned work—he lives his art, lives in it. In 1974 the *National Enquirer* chose Hubbell's home as "Weird House of the Month." Elements that he experimented with at home were later used in the chapel—mosaic motifs incorporated into surfaces, light falling through stained-glass baubles that sprinkle a child's bed with shimmering color, sculptural forms rising from the family pool, magical twists and turns. Every element is lyrical, whimsical, bizarre, as if elemental creatures had been shaping colored air.

Otto Rigan writes in his book *From the Earth Up,* "James and his wife, Anne, see the total creative process of life as a religious one. Reli-

gion permeates all that takes place on their hill and within their lives. This is not doctrinal religion. It is a twenty-four-hours-a-day awareness of a universal order. James' expressions are acts of reverence for that order. There is a religious feeling exposed in James' work that draws upon his faith and Anne's. They live as people who recognize that they are extensions of God, on loan for the short period of a lifetime on earth. They are determined to use the borrowed materials, time, and energy that nature has given them to live the best and most sympathetic lives that nature will allow."

One of Hubbell's most intriguing plans is a proposal for a sculptural underwater home, entitled "Deep Dream," sited three hundred feet off the coast of La Jolla, sixty feet below sea level. One gets the sense that being underwater here would almost be like living in outer space. I can't help but imagine the chapels of the future in both dimensions. Think of the enveloping silence. Many of his more inspired projects have never been realized, but as he says, "To give of love or beauty is not always rewarding in material ways. After all, birds do not get paid to sing." But living the life of the imagination, intent on rendering beautiful things, is a life filled with joy, jubilation.

The desire to create a chapel is in part the desire to merge beauty with ecstasy, to inspire inspiration itself. Hubbell says, "The best of what is called Art is simply communion or worship. The task now is to replant man's soul— the whole of him—into the earth, the sea, and the stars, to remake man in the image of his ancestry, a brother to the universe."

Mother Goddess Altar San Francisco, California

An artistry of acquisition and placement informs Shelley Masters's personal altar. There is nothing "set-up" about it. It looks more like an arrangement that must be continually refreshed, a living bouquet of objects. This heavily curtained shrine room, sponge-painted a deep blue-green, has the feeling of a cave-like environment. Dedicated to the Mother Goddess, her collection borrows from native American Indian traditions as well as various other cultures. There is a sculpture of Kuan-Yin, the Chinese goddess of compassion, as well as a little New Zealand goddess and an Egyptian figure whose egg-shaped head represents the universe. There are three small grandmother statues, which make one think of all that comes in threes—the virgin, matriarch, and crone; the three fates; the trinity. There is also a Matrushka doll, where one little wooden woman opens to reveal a smaller one inside, an apple for Eve, and a statue of Our Lady of Guadalupe.

Dramatic, warm and outgoing, Shelley is eager to talk. She insists that Mexico was once a matriarchal culture, and though Christianity imposed something else on that, they never let go of the Goddess. Raised in a Christian tradition, Shelley always thought of God as "Father," but when she was introduced to the fact that it could also possibly be "Mother," it was somewhat alarming.

She points out the Venus of Willandorf, who is a symbol of fertility and generation. She is all body, faceless, and in that sense represents the transcendent. This figure is placed on a concrete object that Shelley found out in a

151

field, but with the Venus perched on top of it, a hummingbird whirring at an angle below, a curving constellation of stars encircling, there is a feeling of holiness about it.

Shelley goes on to say that before she started working with the shamanistic teacher Michael Harner, she had read over two hundred books concerning saints' experiences and psychedelic experiences. "I would say to myself—

here's some of it—there's a little bit of it—it was as if my hair was on fire.

"My experience of the spirit world is that it's completely unbounded. Manifestation isn't a problem for them—they can do anything quite easily, but in the material world, it takes a big effort. When I ask for help—I might get—*Make yourself these clothes and paint your room this color,* which is not always so easy. In part, I think that's where personal altars come from—each object is an abbreviation of those requests, or an answer encapsulated in a symbol. Maybe if you're not hearing a voice, but you're having a feeling, you call it intuition, and that's safe, but if you're hearing a voice, then it's not safe in our culture. I was experiencing a lot of extra-sensory perceptions, little synchronicities and incidents, but I could still balance my checkbook. I'd hear a voice that might say, *Turn left! Turn left!* and I'd think, Oh come on, I don't need to turn left, I'm going to the store, but I'd try, and then I'd run into someone I hadn't seen for twenty years.

"At one point, I did ask the spirits to stop, and they did, but it was like falling out of bed as a child—everything stopped with a bump, and it was difficult not to have it anymore. I have since learned that when you put a flag up, signaling that you are a spirit-friendly place, they can descend on you—*I want this done, I want that done,* and it can tire you out.

"People want to keep a purist sense of things, but on one of my journeys I found myself confronting the Spirit of the Smile Button, and I'm going—So *gee,* they're all here! The Spirit of the Outboard Motor, the Spirit of the Toaster. When you think about it, a lot of people talk to their cars and even name them. But this put my spiritual arrogance on edge, because we were not just talking about the Big Three, or the Goddess, or Gaia, but also mundane things, like the Spirit of the Camera. All of it. That's the way the Native Americans saw the world. We tend to demonize technology and we elevate the natural, but there is spirit in everything."

Shelley speaks about women and the menstrual cycle, and how our culture demeans that, though it is a cycle of power for women. "Just look at the products—*Stay Free*—get rid of—stay free of what? Society says—treat every single day as if it's exactly the same, and women are forced to deny what's happening to them. I started tracking on a thirteen-moon calendar, and saw that within each month I had creative days, where I was more lucid, organizational days, as well as days of anxiety, which would occur on the sixteenth and seventeenth days of the cycle. On those days I would take on so much work, by the end of my cycle I realized I couldn't do it all. I kept sabotaging myself until I began to recognize the pattern, and then it liberated me."

Wanting to honor the feminine, Shelley got a group of women together. She made a bunch of hearts and dumped baskets of beads, ribbons, and lace out on the floor, and then thirteen women all sat around and made their own heart-shaped creations. Shelley's juicy-looking three-dimensional heart has purple ribbons and golden wings. It is glowing there on her altar, surrounded by sputtering chartreuse candles and a bouquet of orange-red calla lilies. In her group, she says, the women all started to talk like women must have talked at quilting bees in the past, sharing intimate needs, wishes, and desires.

When I ask Shelley about the zebra on her altar, she explains that a zebra has been a main traveling companion on her spiritual journeying and that it took her to the Midnight Circus in Venice. "The performance was lit by torches and candlelight. It was all silks and banners, baroque—exquisite." It seems uncanny that the zebra would be drawn to Venice with its plethora of striped barber poles, dreamy, watery hitching posts for magical creatures such as this.

Shelley began working with Michael Harner in 1994, and she admits that only through this work with him did she learn to communicate effectively. With the monotonous, percussive help of a rattle or drum, which helps to alter consciousness, one can easily learn to journey. Though the phenomenon is somewhat similar to active imagination, Shelley says that she has experienced things that she could never have dreamed up on her own.

She recounts a technique in which one person in the group would mentally go and hide somewhere, and the person next to him would try to find him. "In my journey, I went across the desert and ran up into a tree. I made the tree blossom with different kinds of flowers and I did some gymnastics from a limb—you are very agile in your journeying. Finally, I hung upside down, and saw the Mediterranean. When I came out of my journey, the woman next to me said, 'I'm sorry I didn't find you. I have this new power animal, and it's a bird, and we kept going upside down—finally, at the end, I only saw the sea.' Quite an amazing link, but to me it opens up this other realm. About fifty percent of the couples who were doing this together had some link of success. We use the word *imagination* to cover quite a lot. When somebody says, I *imagine* something, they're really drawing from non-ordinary reality, an idea, a feeling, an inspiration, which is generated from that realm.

Michael Harner writes in *The Way of the Shaman*, "Another important reason that shamanism has wide appeal today is that it is spiritual ecology. In this time of worldwide environmental crisis, shamanism provides a reverence for, and spiritual communication with, the other beings of the Earth and with the Planet itself. In shamanism, this is not simple Nature worship, but a two-way spiritual communication that resurrects the lost connections our human ancestors had with the awesome spiritual power and beauty of our garden Earth."

Shelley says that it is hard for her to step on a bug now. "In fact, it's even hard for me to step on the gas! If I were to step on your toe, and you were to scream in pain, I would know that I had hurt you. But when somebody paves the road, they're not hearing the screaming, because they're not connected to the spirit world. But there's a lot of screaming going on, and when you start to hear it, you can't help but treat your world with more reverence. Everything in life is connected."

Shelley celebrates the four cross-quarters, halfway between the solstices and equinoxes. "Just making a special arrangement on the altar becomes a ritual. One time I felt I needed a piece of sky, so I got a strip of cheesecloth that had blue on it from a time when I painted a cloud ceiling. The silver spoon showed up that way too—something of Mother, domesticity, receptive, a scepter. I only do about two journeys a month now, but they are so sumptuous, with so much going on. In order to remember, I will often find a card or a picture or a carving, and it will find its place for a while on my altar.

"I've come to this as an innocent. I don't think I'd ever call myself a shaman, but this fuels my artwork. Anyone who attempts art opens the door to non-ordinary reality. I believe altars come into existence because if we don't materialize the spiritual realm with these symbols, we forget, and more and more we need to remember. We need to connect."

JERRY WENNSTROM AND MARILYN STRONG

Puget Sound,
Washington

Flaming Stupa

Jerry Wennstrom, "One of the Seven Wonders of Whidbey," is capable of taking the most curious cast-off objects and turning them into art. One would never recognize the old copper commode floats, made into Tibetan-style ornaments with tassels of raffia, hung from the four corners of his prayer tower. Everything he touches he transforms. An unsightly concrete water-holding tank, now covered with ivy, became the base for this most remarkable temple. Water pumps through the meditation space, bubbling up through the petals of a small crystal fountain set before the altar. "The water rises through the fountain sporadically—we never know when," Jerry says, "but it always feels like a blessing."

Ever since I contacted Jerry months ago, we have been in regular correspondence, and already feel like old friends. He is eager to show us the tower, surrounded by tall cedar trees. Light here is precious, and lush gardens take advantage of every patch of sunlight. Jerry has just laid a winding walkway of crushed glass, leading to the tower steps. The path is made from crumbled automobile windshields, but walking upon it gives an odd sensation—a bit like walking on hot coals that miraculously don't burn, or as Jerry might say— "To enter the sacred, you have to walk on broken glass."

At the end of the path there is a metal archway with horseshoes that will soon hold potted plants and wisteria. Beneath this entryway Jerry has laid a plaque with Carl Jung's famous words: *Bidden or unbidden, God is present.*

156

"When we were in Scotland we found a plaque with this saying and Marilyn wanted to buy it, but I said, 'No, let me make one.'"

Jerry had never carved stone before, but then he had never built anything either. He claims the process was magical. He used mostly found or free material, like the two-inch-thick cedar siding, which gives the tower a very solid appearance. Help on the tower also seemed to appear miraculously. One day a group of Sufi practitioners showed up at the perfect moment, wanting to help, and they pulled out all the nails from the heavy boards.

Jerry points out that the tower bell is actually a propane gas tank, the clapper a nozzle. "Everything is junk!" Jerry exclaims. But it is junk in the hands of an alchemist. "I went to the dump in search of something to put on top of the tower, and found these bulbous, brass Indian lamp parts." I admire the stained, carved spiral posts on all four corners of the tower. When nine visiting Tibetan monks saw the fish-bone effect that decorates the roof lines they called it a flaming stupa.

Though Jerry uses the prayer tower often, it was really a gift of love to Marilyn, who is a student of Tsultrim Allione. Marilyn says that she was never drawn to Buddhism before. She had always been more attracted to Celtic earth-based Christianity, but she found Tibetan Buddhism to be very akin to Native American traditions, connecting to the elements. There is also a good deal of focus on the masculine and feminine, which is similar to her Jungian background. "I still consider myself Christian, but I love the Tibetan practices.

They also deal with the darker aspect of the God or Goddess, the wrathful deities, which help you transform whatever negative energies you have."

In a construction method similar to that used for *Yancy Chapel* in Alabama, Jerry rammed old tires with earth to make the gently curving ascent to the meditation space. Just outside the double glass doors, an old copper fire extinguisher has been turned into a prayer wheel. In Tibet the mere spinning of a prayer wheel is spiritually effective, but here I can write down my own personal petition and slip it into the slot before giving the canister a twirl.

The eight-foot-square floor space is covered with blue carpet, comfortable and cozy, but as Jerry points out, "You can look up for thirty-six feet. It's like being inside a steeple." They had to use a crane to mount the top portion of the tower, as it was too precarious for him to build by hand. Jerry points out a little hole in the roof, which is now a birdhouse, with a picture of an owl painted on the side.

If the owl represents "death medicine," as Marilyn tells us, I think Jerry must have been visited a few times. Jerry grew up in a poor black neighborhood in Spring Valley, New York, where many of his young teenage friends died at an early age. "The most beautiful people—the ones we all looked up to—they were the first to go. My best friend ended up getting hepatitis, in jail for robbing taxicabs with a shotgun."

By the 1970s, Jerry was pursuing a career as a young, successful artist, and had acquired a loft space in Nyack, New York. Many of his raw early images, reminiscent of Francis Bacon and Chaim Soutine, delved into the dark side. "I had people literally run out of my studio, they were so disturbed," Jerry admits, "but when Margaret Mead came to my studio, she had a different reaction. She said, 'It's nice to see there is a religious artist emerging in the world.'

"There is often a tendency to deny the dark side," Jerry says, "but there is also something very liberating about facing it. I think if most of us really examine our lives, it was the losses that gave us more of ourselves, not the successes—it was the death experiences."

Around this time, Jerry began to feel that his work had become a false god, and he wanted to give himself to a level of creativity that was more about *being* than doing. It was then that his friend Deborah Koff Chapin took him to meet Hilda Charlton at St. John the Divine. Jerry remembers how Hilda singled him out—"There were probably about one hundred and fifty people there and I was sitting way in the back, but she focused on me, bit this candy, and threw it at me and said, '*Eat it!*'

"After her lecture, I wanted to speak with her, but she flashed this look at me and said, *'Don't talk.'* It was a powerful night. That's all I can say. There were sparks coming out of her ears. If anybody was a saint, who I ever met, it was her. After that I knew I would have to leap into the void. I painted myself out of painting. I wasn't attached to it anymore. It felt like the ultimate creative leap was to destroy my work. It was a very powerful, holy experience that just left me shaken and empty, but exhilarated."

Jerry spent the next ten years living totally by trust. When there was food, he ate. When there wasn't, he fasted. During this time he remained celibate and did not try to make money. "I simply put myself in a position of complete and unconditional service to life, and survived in ways that could only be called miraculous. Your relationship has to be with God, not people. You have to be serving God in each person, and if they give or don't give, that isn't even the issue. *Just give.* I couldn't afford not to be fully present."

In many ways this offering of himself and his artwork was a profound death experience that brought a vital new life along with it. "I gave everything I owned away. I even gave my bed away. One day the owner of my loft space came to me and said, 'Well, you know you are going to have to move,' and I asked him how soon he wanted me to leave, and he said—'As soon as possible,' so I just walked out the door. He was more open-mouthed than I was."

Slowly Jerry started getting back into art by working with kids. And then a Jewish artist and a Catholic nun, who ran the Thorp Intermedia Gallery in the basement of a convent, asked him to participate in a show. As a Christmas gift that year the nuns gave Jerry a little leather purse in the shape of a fish. Only later did he discover that it was full of money. The cash allowed him to travel across country to visit his old friend, Deborah Koff Chapin.

Once on Whidbey Island, Jerry made his way to the Chinook Learning Center, where Marilyn was teaching, and soon they became close. "Marilyn was going through a painful break-up and she didn't really want relationship, and I was celibate, and didn't think I was going in that direction. Because neither of us wanted anything, we could be with each other easily. That was the simple formula."

Today, on the afternoon of our arrival, there is a dedication ceremony planned for a new building at Chinook. We walk a rutted path through the dark, primordial woods to attend. Entering the light-filled building, I look around at the crowd of young, attractive people, and think—did Berkeley die and go to heaven? Each speaker is more articulate and animated than the next.

After the program, I'm introduced to various members of this close-knit community—Jane Hooper, who built an octagonal long dance space with her husband, Kolin; Erica Moseley, who has devoted the third floor of her Victorian home to a Tibetan prayer space; Joy Moulton, a lovely older woman who has a hexagonal ritual space called *Marsh House.* I meet Deborah Koff Chapin, who now runs the *Center for Touch Drawing,* and who introduced me to Jerry in the first place. I begin to feel overwhelmed. When Marilyn suggests that we make our way back to their house, I am ready to slip away.

As we hike through the woods, Marilyn tells us about a program she led called "Gaia Spirit Rising," a women's spirituality program. While Marilyn led these groups with her partner, Renie Hope, Jerry cooked and cleaned and functioned as the only staff person. Jerry also transformed the large open room beneath their living quarters to use as the ritual space, creating shrines and painting murals all around the room. Each one of his unique sculptures creates a different delightful surprise. The stylized form of his artwork makes me think of Egyptian aesthetics, where the underworld is honored, coupled with a carnival-like playfulness that celebrates life.

Marilyn and Jerry are both interested in an earth-based spirituality that is akin to the Native American tradition. "In the Gaia workshops we wanted to help women experience the divine *embodied,* rather than feeling that heaven is out there, that this is a fallen realm and we can do what we please with it. We found that women were hungry for a new kind of inclusive spirituality that was heartfelt and individual."

Gaia is the name the ancient Greeks gave to the Earth Mother, and Marilyn feels that today this archetypal feminine spirit is emerging in different forms all over the world, whether as the Virgin Mary, with her bright blue cloak wrapped around the etheric body of the earth, or as Kali the destroyer. At times she appears as Kuan-Yin, or White Buffalo Calf Woman with her sacred pipe of vision, or Sophia, the Wisdom of the Unknown. Marilyn says that the Jungian analyst Marion Woodman even went so far as to say, "What we await in the Second Coming is actually the emergence of the feminine side of God." Perhaps that is the Zeitgeist of our times.

In keeping with their interest in Native American spirituality, Marilyn and Jerry also have a sweat lodge in their lower garden. It is only about four feet high, which to me seems claustrophobic. Marilyn says that the experience in the sweat lodge is often about facing one's fears—"You don't know whether you can survive it. You feel like you might suffocate or die of heat prostration. You open up in a new way when you are that humbled."

"It's very *very* powerful," Jerry adds. "I have fasted for a month, and I have to say, that one bout in the sweat lodge puts you in the same place. I mean you are just *leveled* with the earth—you are so wide open."

It is hard to imagine Jerry being any more open, for as the poet David Whyte says in a new film about Jerry's life: "One of the most magnificent things about Jerry is his profound and courageous innocence. He has created a tremendous friendship with a part of himself, which is in love with the world, and his artistry displays that. Jerry is one of the few people I know who, in a very quiet way, has actually claimed his happiness in existence."

Months ago, when I first contacted Jerry, it was the day after he had completed work on the meditation tower. The timing was so auspicious, he was jubilant— "This feels like a christening phone call!" I was not surprised, for so much of this book has had that quality of blessed synchronicity.

Later Jerry writes to me:

> We had the most wonderful event. Nine Tibetan monks from the Depung Loseling Monastery came here and did a consecration blessing in our stupa. All nine of them piled into the eight-foot square tower. They chanted, rang bells, did chod drum, threw rice and water, all in a forty-five minute ritual, to bless our humble tower! The tower glowed for three days following the event. So did my heart!
>
> We then had a banquet downstairs in our other "temple" where the monks played with everything. There are lots of bells and whistles and mechanical things to interact with, which they did in the most childlike way. The "performance" they did was quite simply powerful. They fall right into ritual space. I do believe that is how they are able to continue this two-year tour. They hold to the sacred. I hope your journey continues to keep your own heart full. Love & Blessings, Jerry

Marilyn and Jerry's tower was subsequently consecrated by a Native Siberian Shaman, "Nadyezhda," the wisdom keeper of the Ulche tribe. She was participating in a local conference on indigenous peoples, but had time to come bless their tower and house with great quantities of vodka, some of which they were instructed to drink.

"Nadyezhda requested two small glasses for the blessing," Jerry recalls, and not realizing that the glasses would be filled to the brim, to symbolize abundance, Marilyn gave her champagne flutes. "That was one fast road to heaven! I guess I'm very American in the *more is better* attitude toward blessings on our land and tower," Jerry admits. Indeed, can one have too many blessings? And can one truly give, without having received them?

The Moonlodge Northern New Mexico

Inspired by the circular kivas of Pueblo Indians as well as the Neolithic cave sanctuaries found at Catal Huyuk, a women's spirituality group in northern New Mexico decided to create their own ceremonial space. A backhoe could have made short work of the digging process, but the group was committed to creating this space by themselves. The laborious, awesome process, often done under high-altitude sun, bonded the group in a profound way. Together, over the course of three years, on weekends and in their spare time, they began to move the earth.

Though winter storms eroded the walls and work had to begin anew each spring, finally the diameter of the hole expanded to a satisfying twenty-four feet, and then shovels were replaced by picks and jackhammers as the women worked their way down to the level of bedrock.

Various members described their feelings about the making of the temple in an essay published by WOMAN OF POWER. Barbara wrote, "Down in the hole, with brilliant blue sky and sunshine for a ceiling, I wondered what impulse was behind this undertaking. A primeval urge, perhaps, to burrow in, to feel enveloped, embraced by clay and stone. An instinct to worship by going down and within rather than up and out."

Another woman aptly spoke of the creation of this evolving womb-like space as "feminine vernacular architecture." The elegant curves do seem to want to speak the language of women alone with each other, laughing and praising.

Mary, an experienced builder, admitted that she was afraid of the depth

163

of the pit at first, the darkness of the close quarters. It was only when the *vigas* were peeled and raised skyward that she responded. "The beams all support each other in a circle, the bearing weight resting equally on all—a community of timber reflecting our community of women."

Most of the labor up to this point had been donated, but now there was a need to purchase materials. In the winter of 1988–89, a member of the group was diagnosed with cancer and died within months, leaving the group a bequest toward the completion of the roof. With her loss, the group felt an even greater need for their sacred space, where they could take their grief and prayers.

Mary and Nancy Jane took on the task of constructing the exterior subroof of plywood, tarpaper, and shingles, an intricate process, moving from the interior spiral shape to the exterior octagonal frame around the skylight. When they were ready to plaster the interior of the structure with mud and straw, patting and smoothing the local mud onto the earthen walls, one member admits to going to the work party out of a sense of obligation, but soon she was taking a ball of wet mud in her hands, pressing it flat and throwing it against the curving surface before smoothing it out with bare palms. Jamie wrote, "As I massaged and kneaded the mud into the wall, giving the temple a skin, covering her bones, I began enjoying myself. It was like being a kid."

All of a sudden a number of people got inspired. DeAnn said that she would carve a moon door, and Joy agreed to make the stained glass window. Anita wanted to create the fireplace as a kachina-mother archetype. With the help of her daughter she built the primary structure out of fire-resistant masonry blocks. "I made a clay image of *La Guadalupeña* and etched a message on it, put it on the smoke shelf, and built around it. It is a prayer for the protection of the females in my family and our loved ones. That's how powerful I felt this lodge to be and how powerfully it affected me."

Anita's Great Mother fireplace makes *The Moonlodge* come alive. The perfectly round opening and swollen belly shape of this exquisite earthen sculpture makes one think of pregnancy and birth, being *in the round*, all the circles women encompass during that time of gestation, swollen breasts and belly, the dilating cervix, the fire of birth pain that we must pass through.

The big swollen shape of the fireplace is a nurturing presence in *The Moonlodge*—all eyes are on its portal as the piñon wood crackles, throwing out considerable heat. Ledges for votive candles are incorporated into the whole, and curving *bancos* of varying heights embrace the roaring furnace. There is something about gathering around the hearth light of an open fire that instinctively brings people together to tell their stories and to sing their songs.

"Our first miracle, our first brilliance," Jean tells us, "was when we decided to have a rotational leadership. At first it felt as if we were sacrificing depth, because we weren't doing the same thing over and over again. But I don't feel that way anymore." As each one of the members takes turns leading, bringing a variety of ceremonies and spiritual practices, the group tries to honor whatever differences arise.

At times the group has run into problems. One member had trouble dealing with anything Christian or Jewish. "It was the Wednesday before Good Friday, and someone asked another to talk about the Stations of the Cross, and this particular woman was appalled that she would have to deal with such patriarchal things. The rest of us, who had been around longer, knew that tolerance was our most sacred premise. We went ahead and did the Stations of the Cross, and it was a difficult moment. Since then, this same woman has done some reconciliation with her Jewish background. She has made her peace somehow.

"A lot of times we seem to cycle," Jean explains. "We'll have a year when we are really into music, and then we'll start moving someplace else. We had a couple of times when I got annoyed, because I thought everybody was just into—*laughing*. I wanted us to remember that we were there to do practice, not just to be a happy family. I felt the family aspect was a fringe benefit, but I did not see it as the central reason for us being together. What I've learned over the years is that whenever one of us steps forward to say what's going to happen in the space, it's only a matter of making a vessel. We have enough trust in each other at this point.

"Whether somebody is skillful or not is not what makes an evening feel successful. What is successful is when someone leads from her own need, which means she is relating from her vulnerability rather than from authority. Then it really doesn't matter how clumsy somebody is. We learned that by trial and error, and we'll follow that forever."

I ask Jean if gay spirituality has something unique about it, and she says she feels that it does. She believes the lesbian population has a certain anguish-defiance that rejects authority. "If we weren't defiant, we would never have bothered to become gay. We would have found a way to conform. Any spiritual authority becomes immediately suspect. I know I can't shake it. I am a fundamentalist preacher missionary's daughter. I see someone in a costume and I react. I am not willing to give authority over to anyone."

A few years into the project, Jean learned a piece of her own story concerning incest and sexual abuse. In times of great distress, she would descend the ramp into the belly of *The Moonlodge* and sit there until she was able to relax. "I wondered, is this temple the place that will transform my shame, and the shame of my mother? To me, God is an infinite web of energy that encompasses all life."

I ask her about her relationship with her family now. How do they feel about what she is doing? Do they accept her? She responds, "My father, by the time he died, was willing to say—'I see that you are a spiritual being, even if you are not doing it the way I wish you would.' I'm not sure my mother ever did believe that. My mother just died a month ago, and I did experience her death as a release. That's one of the passages that our group is doing, because many of our parents are dying. We're all croning at the same time. We're all getting cranky together."

On the night of our visit to *The Moonlodge,* Cathy has chosen to lead a forgiveness ceremony inspired by Yom Kippur. Around seven o'clock, just as the sun is about to set, the group comes trailing in. Everyone is warm and friendly.

We begin the evening ceremony by standing in a circle together. "We come together tonight to celebrate this community, to give thanks for this day and to become present to the moment. Take a few seconds to reflect on the day, and another few seconds to remember those who have passed on. Remember those right now who are stressed. We also remember the new babies who have just come into the world, and send them love and light.

"The high Jewish holiday of Yom Kippur was on Wednesday," Cathy continues, "and ten days before that was Rosh Hashanah, which means—new beginning. It is a time of repentance, a time to ask for forgiveness, and to give forgiveness. We can do that even if we are unaware of having offended someone—we can still ask for forgiveness. In forgiving and being forgiven we free up life energy and are written in the Book of Life for another year. Another thought about atonement at the personal level—it is not until we forgive others, and probably also forgive ourselves, only when we start at that individual level, that we are then able to heal the world. So I think Yom Kippur is an amazing holiday.

"I had thought of us each asking forgiveness from each other, but I think I'd rather begin with collective forgiveness. I brought a prayer from Michael Lerner, *Atonement for the Collective People* from *Tikkun* magazine. It begins in Yiddish. Is there is anybody who would like to try reading it? April?"

April replies, "*Aloha.* That's all I know, Hawaiian Yiddish." Everybody laughs. It is clear that this group is comfortable together and that they like to have a good time. Cathy suggests that we each take turns reading the prayer, and she begins:

> For all our sins, may the Force that makes forgiveness possible, forgive us, pardon us, and make atonement possible.
>
> For the sins we have committed before you and in our communities by being so preoccupied with ourselves, that we ignore the larger problems of the world in which we live;
>
> And for the sins which we have committed by being so directed toward outward realities that we ignored our own spiritual development;
>
> For the sins of accepting the current distribution of wealth and power as unchangeable;
>
> And for the sins of giving up on social change and focusing exclusively on personal advancement and success;
>
> For the sins of feeling so powerless when we hear about oppression that we finally close our ears;
>
> For the sins of dulling our outrage at the continuation of poverty, oppression, and violence in this world . . .
>
> For the sin of accepting a world in which the "bottom line" is money and power, and not fighting for a new bottom line of love and caring;
>
> And for the sin of being cynical about the possibility of building a world based on love;
>
> And for the sin of spreading negative stories about people we know;
>
> And for the sin of listening and allowing others to spread negative stories . . .
>
> For these sins we ask God and each other to give us the strength to forgive ourselves and each other . . .

Hearing this meditation, I am reminded of how important it is to renew our social consciousness, a traditional concern for modern Jews, dealing with problems and injustices in the world. I am also reminded of how much we need to instruct our children, through example, not to lead self-indulgent, narrow lives, but to do for others, to be as generous as possible, not only to cultivate attitudes of tolerance, but to show active compassion for the poor.

Standing in a circle before the blazing fire, Cathy asks Jamie to instruct us in a ritual dance set to music. Jamie shows us how to use our knees to push ourselves forward. Making a crescent moon, using our hearts as the fulcrum, we make a slight bow—the swaying keeps going in the same direction, one step for each phrase.

This group is vocally gifted. They easily pick up the song—*Abwoon D'Bashmaya,* which is the original Aramaic of what Jesus would have said in the Lord's Prayer: *Our Father Who Art in Heaven.* But Aramaic is a very fluid, vocal language, with lots of layers of meanings and levels of sound. Another translation might be: *O Birther of the Universe from whom the breath of life comes.* There is a counterpoint in the song—the names of God in Aramaic, Arabic, Hebrew, and Old Canaanite: *Allaha, Allah, Elohim, Elat.* "You can hear how close the names of God are in all those languages," Cathy reminds us.

As we begin singing, I feel as if I am taken back into Old Jerusalem with this group of women, feeling the power of ancient song. My Jewish ancestors, Levi and Mordecai Sheftall, raise their heads and listen. Ironically, the creation of *The Moonlodge* began with the idea of making a space where women could go when they were bleeding, though menstruation was considered taboo in the temple during Old Testament times. But now we are gathered here together, dancing in a circle, trying not to raise too much dust, repeating over and over this holy chant, a beautiful interweaving of tones as we sway and move around the circle.

When we finally come to a standstill, the group sings a Hebrew song: *Shema Israel Adonai Elohanu, Adonai Echod—Listen, Oh you who struggle with the Infinite, All is One.* Then settling back down on the curving *bancos,* each woman shares an experience she's had here in *The Moonlodge.*

Through the years, various traditions have developed, and one of them is the Day of the Dead. "That has always been a very strong highlight for me. I remember we created this gorgeous graveyard that was all decorated with flowers in the cold crisp wind."

Another woman talks about making papier-mâché statues of Harriet Tubman, St. Brigid, Aung San Sui Kyi, and Our Lady of Guadalupe. "We took them out for a parade. I always think, Oh my God, what are the neighbors thinking!"

"Sometimes we all sit on the teeter-totter and try to balance each other on the equinox."

"And we get into *big* fights sometimes. You can't be close unless you fight. After thirteen years the honeymoon wears off, and you start questioning—Are we even spiritually compatible?!"

"We thought about changing the name from moonlodge, but we couldn't. We are lunitarians. *Lunatics,*" they laugh.

"One of the things that I love the most about our group is its diversity, the variety of people who have been here and who have left or who have visited. I think about how many times we've met every single week for all these years, the number and variety of experiences, from the sublime to the ridiculous."

"One year Jamie got real fired up from singing in the gospel choir at the Michigan Women's Music Festival, and so we sang all these spirituals. Remember that? We had a choir for a while. It was great. I think we did remarkably well. And then what was really magical, was when we did chanting for a while, and we could not decide what to sing. So we put everybody's favorite chant into a hat—we were going to do four—and each one was from a different tradition. That was amazing."

The Moonlodge collective has a feeling of familiarity. The space they've created has a comfortable, well-lived-in, well-loved look, but there is also a special feeling of reverence. As Kat says, "There is something about the sheer presence of earth in that circle that affirms what is true and shatters what is not. *The Moonlodge* is emerging as a transformational force in our lives, in ways we have yet to learn."

HANNE AND MAURICE STRONG'S

Crestone, Colorado # Manitou AND

BARBARA AND WILLIAM HOWELL'S

Sanctuary House

On a curving retaining wall at the ashram in Crestone, we see a painting of an angel pulling a long banner of emblems from all the different world religions, streaming along together in one glorious whole. This could be the signature banner for this entire community, *Manitou*, where all the great world religions are represented. Though I have not been able to give equal representation to all the traditions, I would like to wrap such a ribbon around our book, for this collection has a similar spirit of intention, just as many of the small chapel owners included have had a similar impulse—to gather together.

Those who worship here at the ashram are followers of Babaji, who felt that all religions lead to God—*I don't care what religion you practice, just do it.* Donna and I have arrived just in time for a *navratri* ceremony in honor of the Divine Mother. This fire ceremony, one of the oldest Vedic traditions, is intended to purify not only the participants but the surrounding area as well. Though we have arrived a bit late, we follow the sound of chanting voices up toward the fire pit, where a lovely blond woman, Ramloti, is reading prayers in Sanskrit and Hindi. The seated group around the fire pit responds repeatedly with—"*Swaha,*" tossing offerings of *samagri* into the crackling fire. Perfumed incense rises into the juniper-scented air. In the bright mountain sunlight, I find myself intoxicated by the sensual aspects of the ceremony—the perfumed smoke, the marigold garlands, the rhythms of cymbals, bells, and drums, the conch shells sounding, an eerie haunting music that fills my soul with longing.

170

Many have been on a partial fast these past nine days of *navratri,* and a feeling of elation permeates the group as we head down to the lower garden for a vegetarian feast—everything is beautiful and delicious. Today at the ashram, the children are being presented with a bag of precious gifts, silk turbans for the boys, head scarves for the girls, as well as candy and other presents to acknowledge the Divine presence within each one of them. For the moment they are little kings and queens.

Apparently, very few of the people in attendance would call themselves Hindus—there are actually more Catholics and Buddhists, but the community here on the Baca Grande tries to honor various celebrations together as much as possible. I am drawn to this open, tolerant attitude. It doesn't change my basic beliefs, but it doesn't offend them either. In this same ecumenical spirit different guests offer their blessings —an Israeli song, a Cree Indian chant, as well as a song for Mary—*Oh beautiful mother, my heart is on fire, to love and to serve you, is my only desire.*

As the day winds down, we decide to take advantage of the approaching sunset and head off to photograph Najeeb Halaby's prayer tower at the far end of the Baca Grande. This yellow-ochre prayer tower seen from a distance looks like an ancient Assyrian ziggurat. Halaby remembers one inspiring moment when a whole flock of bluebirds flew over the tower, almost taking his breath away. He goes on to tell us that his daughter, Noor, embraced Islam when she married the late King Hussein of Jordan. Halaby is proud of the fact that his daughter was much more than a figurehead, but a working queen with many active social concerns.

Facing the grand San Luis Valley, with the towering peaks of the Sangre de Cristos behind, the prayer tower stands in an inspiring location. A storm front is moving north from New Mexico. Sheets of rain and lightning are visible in the distance. Sunlight breaks through huge cloud formations, streaking across the plain. The mountains behind us, with their canyons of saffron-colored aspen, change guises as quickly as a troupe of actors playing multiple parts, austere and forbidding one moment, grand and welcoming the next.

We take our time ascending the path to the ziggurat as the sandy earth gives way beneath our feet. At the summit, we are overcome, as the late light brightens the rich yellow-ochre against the deep blue of early evening. It is magnificent. I can imagine the religious leaders of the Baca Grande standing around the ramp-like ascent of the ziggurat, offering their blessings and prayers of thanks, like different sections in some great orchestra, united by the same big drum.

The following day we drive slowly down a rough dirt road to the Mountain Zen Center. Richard Baker-Roshi is away, but we take the liberty of looking at the Lindisfarne Chapel, now part of the Zen Center complex. It was the first piece of sacred architecture built here on the Baca. Lindisfarne, a contemplative community of scholars, has offered seminars in sacred geometry since the late seventies, and many of the people originally involved with this chapel were absorbed in that study.

The inspiration for the space initially came to William Thompson as a circle in which the facets were elliptical petals of Dante's multi-foliate rose. "I saw a person seated on each of the petals, equally oriented toward the center. In my crude sketches I tried to show how the seventy-two petals would exfoliate from the central altar, a simple millstone with a large candle. . . . The chapel was to be the portal between time and eternity."

Beginning with the top and working down, Keith Critchlow worked out a design for the roof with structural engineers. Twelve interweaving support beams make the interior resemble the inside of a basket. The group agreed on the Cistercian dictum: *No decoration, only proportion,* so that people of any faith would feel comfortable within the space. "With religious sects battling each other all over the world," Thompson writes, "it meant all the more to look around and see a Rabbi, a Sufi Sheikh, an Anglican Bishop, a Quaker, a Zen Buddhist Roshi, and a Cistercian Priest, all seated together in silent meditation. Each honored the tradition of the other and each followed the path of his or her own traditional culture into the silence that was around and above all cultures and tradition."

Just yards away, the Japanese-style zendo is a strictly maintained space. Everything is done in a very exact way, which can make it slightly awkward for the uninformed visitor. As we exchange our day shoes for traditional temple slippers, Katrin, one of the people living at the center, unlocks the door, and then we understand why they want to guard the perfection of the place—every detail has been rendered with such skill, using only the finest materials. Four huge paper globes help to illuminate the room and small windows let in a bit of afternoon light, but basically, the rectangular space is guarded from any harshness, lending itself to a soothing serenity of mind.

In contrast to this minimal aesthetic, Tibetan Buddhism seems more colorful and cluttered, more feminine. Hanne Strong's house, at the bottom of Moonlight Drive, is like a museum of artifacts from all over the world, with huge carved Tibetan guard dogs and hanging tankas. In a previous incarnation Hanne was an interior designer, and this talent is obvious in her shrine room upstairs, painted a deep rich red and filled with an abundance of personal treasures.

Hanne's history goes back to the beginning of *Manitou.* In 1978, three months after the Strongs arrived in Crestone, a wild-haired man known by locals as "the prophet" came out of the hills and told Hanne that she would gather all the great world religions together here so that they could reside in harmony during this time of spiritual purification. Ancient Indian tribes had always considered this high agricultural valley to be one of the great sacred centers of the world. Peaceful counsel and healing ceremonies took place here. Blood was never shed.

The Strongs acquired an enormous piece of property on the Baca Grande, and though the prophet's words had resonance, Hanne wasn't sure what to do until she went on a four-day retreat up in the mountains. Then the prophecy was confirmed. "The spirits told me—*You're not coming off this mountain until*

you've laid the entire vision out. So that's how the map emerged. And when I walked off the mountain, the first person I met was the architect I used to draw up the plans."

Hanne says that when she started *Manitou,* she knew that she had to understand the essence of each great religion. She studied the Native American way—shamanism, and lived in a Zen monastery in Japan. She also spent five years with a Hindu Brahmin priestess, Sheila Devi, who was sent here by Babaji. When I ask where Sheila is now, Hanne responds, "On the other side. She fell off a horse and died here. She was a real horsewoman, but if your time is up, it's up. Bottom line!" Hanne has an almost raucous sense of humor that is startling and yet earthy. She is not reverential, but generous and friendly, encouraging us to stay for supper.

The Strongs continue to give large land grants to various religious groups. Just this week Hanne will be meeting with an African elder for a school on the spiritual tradition of the Congo. They are also establishing the *Buffalo Trust* here, which will house the main national archives for Native Americans, a place where elders can disseminate knowledge to young people in direct oral transmission. Pulitzer Prize winning author N. Scott Momaday will be in charge of this venture. "When he saw this land his eyes just lit up. You can look for a hundred miles and never see another building. There's nothing else like it."

In the backyard of Hanne's house, there is a Native American fire circle. I'm delighted to hear that it is the creation of Ra Paulette, who sculpted the sandstone cathedral near Ojo Caliente. Suddenly the world seems like a very small place. I feel as if the connections we've made in this book are beginning to spiral—if we kept on going, we might come back to the beginning. It is a pleasure to admire Ra's work. Around the fire pit are eight stone seats, while the floor of the circle is composed of pink granite slabs with dark green travertine details. Arrow shapes of stone point to the four directions, a buffalo skull looks toward the east, and Tibetan prayer flags ripple in the wind.

One might call *Manitou* an Earth Spirit endeavor. The Strongs have put into motion various ecological farm projects: the Ethnobotany Institute for the collection and preservation of medicinal and food plants from around the world; a community seed bank that gathers heirloom seed from the valley as well as hardy seed varieties from other zones. Hanne is very concerned with involving youth in earth restoration and hopes to organize a big music concert for peace that will ignite the passions of the young.

In 1980 the Strongs gave 200 acres to the sixteenth Kamapa, of the Gyalwa lineage. When the Kamapa came to the Baca Grande, he had a very strong sense that this would be the place where the rich legacy of Tibetan Buddhism could be passed on to future generations. A year later he passed away, and it was decided that the stupa would be dedicated to him.

A stupa is believed to radiate the essence of enlightenment, and has the power to transform consciousness. Certainly the seven years it took to create this stupa must have transformed the inner lives of Maria Pelaez, a Venezuelan, Mark Elliott, an Englishman, and Marianne Marstrand, Hanne Strong's younger sister from Denmark. Numerous members of the community participated in the construction of the stupa and helped to make the 100,000 *tsa-tsa*s (each a symbolic representation of the Buddha himself), but it was the persistent dedication of these three followers who saw the project through.

A discerning monk chose the location for the stupa. He felt that the placement in the foothills of the Sangre de Cristos was perfect, not only because of the surrounding mountains and rivers, but because it was also in the center of the country and rested on top of one of the largest aquifers in America. When the monk rose from the selected spot, he said, "The land's eye, *here.*" And indeed, one senses that the window of the soul of this site must be reflecting the heavens above.

The first objects to be set inside the stupa's foundation were weapons of all kinds, as the stupa is meant to quell conflict. The lamas instructed the builders to then fill the base with juniper and treasure vases that held mandalas and mantras, along with musical instruments, medicines, herbs, food, jewels and perfumes, silver and gold. In part because the Chinese had destroyed so many stupas in Tibet, the Crestone group was able to acquire a large number of holy relics to place in the *Tashi Gomang Stupa.*

It is believed that the power of the stupa helps to maintain positive energy, subduing the negative, not only locally, but throughout the country. During the dedication ceremony Bokar Rinpoche visualized all negative actions in a plate of blackened sesame seed, which was then burnt and purified.

175

"To embrace with a loving heart," he said, "goes beyond all nationalities, goes beyond the notion of religion altogether. A loving experience of our commonalities, that is the experience of the celebration."

When Maria Pelaez comes to meet me at the home of Barbara Howell, she gives me a packet of the seeds used during the consecration, a very special gift. I will take the packet home and put the seeds into the altar of Little Rose Chapel.

Barbara and William Howell are in the midst of creating a circular retreat space called *Sanctuary House,* with meditation rooms dedicated to the four great traditions—Jewish/Christian, Buddhist, Hindu/Vedic and Sufi/Muslim, all of which will surround a central labyrinth garden, based on the great labyrinth in Chartres Cathedral. Of all the holy personal places on the Baca, this venture seems to capture the spirit of *Manitou*—a microcosm of the bigger plan.

Barbara and I settle down on a floor mat in the Jewish/Christian room, which has just been completed. "This was not going to be the final altar," Bar-

bara says of the large grey stones, "but William went up the road and found these rocks a few weeks ago, and now I'm so in love with it, I think we are going to leave it." William also peeled the timbers, which support the ceiling. A mild wax covers the hard-packed earthen floor, and a special sealer called okan covers the smoothed adobe surface of the walls.

Barbara and William converted to Catholicism twelve years ago while living in British Columbia. "I started having this inner feeling, this inner experience that I absolutely couldn't explain—something was just growing. Though we didn't feel ready, we entered the Church at Easter Vigil. A Vietnamese priest had taken over, and he sensed that I was having a mystical experience that night. I almost passed out into the baptismal font, and he came over and held my hand and he had a tear in his eye. The Holy Spirit just took me over—it reoriented my entire life.

"We went to live in Snowmass, to spend time with Father Thomas Keating, who I just love so dearly—it's a very progressive community there. We had already found that there was an essential wonderful truth in all the traditions. My experience saw it immediately, no separation. When you have been hit by the Divine, there is only one Divine, in many expressions. We were at a conference with Father Keating in California called *Harmonium Mundi*. It was the day the Dalai Lama won the Nobel Peace Prize, and he was there as the main speaker, and it knocked my head off, it really did—we were just in love with each one of the speakers. I think we realized then that it was the mystical side of each tradition that we were drawn to."

The Howells began to visit Crestone, and then someone donated the land for *Sanctuary House*, and they received a large grant for the building. Barbara admits that it has all been a miraculous journey, even though their lives do not seem to make rational sense. "We went to India two years ago and found this yogi saint in the jungle. He was this extraordinary, fully realized soul, and he said, 'I've walked many times with your Lord Jesus.' And I just felt my heart break wide open, and then I had a vision of Christ there, and when I came back and asked Father Thomas—what on earth—why would it be, that I would go to India, in this little ashram in the middle of the jungle with this yogi saint and have such a profound experience of Christ, and he said, 'Well, why not? One can not localize Christ.' And so I wept."

Not many people can follow a path like this. Most people have to plant their roots very deeply, in one given faith, but perhaps Barbara and William were given such a profound experience so that they could recognize it elsewhere. Joining William in the house, Barbara begins to make cookies for the evening dedication ceremony. They have invited me to come back and join a group of Carmelite friends from the nearby *Spiritual Life Institute*, who will lead the blessing on the new room. Someday soon *Sanctuary House* will offer retreat apartments to visiting guests, just as the Carmelites and Buddhists do now. Silence and contemplation seem to be a big part of the desert experience.

"It's amazing we live here," Barbara acknowledges, and William adds, "It's amazing that we live anywhere." There is surely something in this high desert plain, something in the earth or open air, that makes one feel amazed here, alternately jubilant then strangely weepy—broken open, grateful to be alive.

Little Rose Chapel Dedication

After a miserable stretch of cold and ragged weather, today opens with a special radiance—the sky is blue and warm and clear. I want to hold my breath and make it last, make it hold. I know this day is special, the way a wedding day is special, with a certain anxious anticipation that comes before any new beginning.

For days we have carried around checklists. Earlier this week I scrubbed and sealed the marble floor and then painted the interior stucco a warmer white. The chemicals temporarily masked the rosy incense smell that had permeated the walls, but only time can retrieve that now. Mason has worked especially hard on carving the rake boards with a curving vine and finishing the wooden niche around the Torcello statue.

Em notes how the painted blue background within the niche makes you feel as if Mary were standing before the sea. The last of the gold leaf is used to gild the interior of her arch, which will pick up candlelight from either side. I have saved two special candles from New Mexico, with gold dove emblems, for this occasion. The tiny pinch-pot bowl Em gave Ayler for graduation will hold Mary's miniature bouquet.

Em arrives at the house with a basket of herbs and pansies to decorate the bases of the hurricane lamps for the long deck table. "Rosemary is for the Virgin," she whispers, as if she too is in on this now. It is so wonderful to have her help and support. Each herb, she points out, has some biblical reference. She tells me not to worry about the scuzzy blooms from the sunburst locust, dropping their litter on the white tablecloth.

I have just framed a favorite photograph of my friend Tadea with her grand-mother, and arranged a special niche for her in the chapel with a conical mother-of-pearl shell, a small Venetian blue glass bottle holding holy water from Lourdes, as well as the jeweled cross I bought from an Indian woman in southern Arizona. I had wanted to give this cross to Tadea when she was ill, but couldn't quite part with it. I loaned the same cross to my father in the hospital, and remember him holding it, how his illness stripped both of us down to a place where we needed prayer, needed help, and it was given.

A freshly ironed linen cloth is draped over the altar with a circular piece of fine lace from my great-grandmother's attic. I place fresh beeswax candles all around, arranging full bouquets of peachy-cream roses in both side niches—they are opening now to a luscious fullness. The Bambino de Prague *is perched on my great-aunt Isabelle's blue silk box, placed before the golden cross that Mason made. I put the lamb fetish I bought at the Chimayó trading post on one of the smooth stones I found on the beach in Door County and set it down by the Infant's feet. I realize that the experiences from our various trips all around the country have come together for me here.*

Everything looks beautiful and feels just right, though I'm sure there will be surprises. I don't even know how many people are coming. Calls keep coming in. Luckily, I have Ayler and Aimé to help me, and they have been diligent, cleaning the rock pool of its winter leaves, washing windows inside and out, setting up tables and carrying coolers, sweeping the endless sunburst locust debris from the deck.

As I've been forewarned, my father arrives exactly at three, but I am still in the bathtub. I do feel especially grateful for his presence here today, grateful for his recovered health. His last CAT scan showed that the dark area in his lung had not only stabilized, it had completely reversed itself. Good news good news good news. Of all the people I have to thank for this chapel, I end my list with him—for in my heart, I dedicate this little place of worship to him as well as to St. Thérèse, who has showered us both with roses.

I feel such gratitude for Mason and all he has done to bring this chapel to life. Each person comes to faith in his own way, and his has been by physically making—carving the holy water font out of a hunk of marble, building the cross from a two-by-four and gilding it by hand, smoothing the stucco up on the curving walls—every bit of it a gift of love, and yet he is self-effacing, and won't let me list his name on the program with everyone else who has helped.

Anne Fredericks arrives with the plaque she's been working on—an image of a descending dove, flying down with a rose over the October 1st sky—St.

Thérèse's feast day, a night when both Pegasus and Andromeda shine. The dark delphinium blue of the egg tempera makes the gold of the streaming light luminous. We hold the plaque over the holy water font, mark the spot for hanging it with a burnt match, hoping that Mason will manage one more small feat before the ceremony begins.

A car pulls up—it's Father Peter, and it is only four o'clock! I'm still in my shorts. "You're early!" I cry, thinking—no more time—this day is running away with me. But after a few introductions, he is happy to wander about by himself while I get dressed.

White cabbage roses arrive from Philip Pahner—"Exultate Jubilate," and another bouquet from Kenny Buchanan, a childhood friend. Ayler cuts the grilled flank steak and lays it out on a platter of cilantro. I need a cup of strong black tea and offer Father a glass of bubbly water. We sit together on the deck and look over the program. He seems more approachable than usual, in a jovial, amicable mood.

"I had to write to get permission to do this, you know," he informs me. "I told the bishop it was just a small, private shrine, not for public use. So don't get me into trouble," he laughs. He has brought his censer for incense, and an aspergillum, a whisk broom made of hyssop, which he uses to spray holy water about. I want him to give us all a good dousing. He seems happy sitting out on the deck, wandering down to pat the horses. I overhear him as he walks out around the little pools of the rock garden—"I love this house," and I feel blessed. It is such a beautiful spot.

Everyone is amazed by the day we've been given. Donna comes flying up the drive with Elaine, her Jamaican friend. Ernie and Faye Santoro arrive. It is their fifty-fifth wedding anniversary. They have brought two other women along, and Faye has her wonderful sour cream bundt cake in a basket. More and more people begin to arrive, carrying delicious-looking plates of food. But I am only thirsty. Nervous? Ayler is in charge of greeting guests and parking cars. I only wish that my son Clovis were here. Vikki True, the gospel singer, arrives and wants to go out to the chapel to practice with Melinda Gardner, who has come with Tadea's harp. Tadea's daughter, Sarah, walks up the driveway, and informs me, "That woman is wearing my dress," but I tell Sarah that she looks particularly good, with her gardening suntan and turquoise feather earring.

Helen, my cousin, appears on time, which alone is a small miracle. She helps me carry the rugosa rose petals out to the chapel. Their fresh perfume rises from the heat of the baskets, delicious, intoxicating. I want to bury my face in the bright pink petals. Nancy Neuman peeks in. She has brought me a candle from Fatima. The five of us stand in a circle and sing rounds of "Jubilate Deo"—

180

amazing how the sound fills this small space with such resonance, magnifying the dimensions.

As friend Stella once said, "Oh, the chapel goes way beyond you," and I responded, "That's for sure!" with such affirmation we both had to laugh. Now I stand back amazed, and realize how this chapel is like a child whom I can admire apart from myself. I feel so comfortable here, knowing each little nook, each personal detail—the nautilus shell we brought back from Kauai, the pink crystal cross Anne found in Bisbee, the Russian icon from Barbara and Pedro when they went to get Vanya, their adopted son, above the door the retablo *of St. Thérèse made by Manny Gurule. The chapel already has a life of its own, and this is simply her christening day.*

I have stored kitchen matches in the clay container Ayler made in ceramics class at school. He carved a cross in the unbaked clay and then fired the pot to a creamy matte yellow. It has a little lid with carving all over it. Lighting the round beeswax candle in the hanging lantern above, I also illuminate a few of the larger candles, then rush back to the house to greet guests who are gathering on the lawn now within the walls of the front garden. The sun is shining and warm and yet there isn't a single blackfly or mosquito to bother us.

Jill helps me pass the programs out. Her friendship of over thirty years has a special quality—she is my touchstone, always there at the most important moments in my life, the least important, too. Her astonishing dark purple iris and blue delphinium are displayed in the entrance. As always she has given her best. Mason has been mowing the fields, and everything looks well-groomed. The day itself has that feeling of ripeness, readiness. People are still arriving, but we are ready to go. I ask Father Peter to lead us.

I can hear Melinda playing the harp as we approach the chapel in a long line, winding up the hill around the birch trees. Thank goodness we didn't take down the crooked little apple tree—for me it represents the soul of this place. People cluster at the door to gaze in, before continuing around to the north side where the ground is level. Here we will gradually plant our woodland sanctuary with shad blow, sea foam roses, and shasta viburnum. The bench with the curved back I gave Mason for his birthday is there for Em and Milt and my father to sit on. I wish I had set up more chairs for the older people in attendance. I notice Bernie Krainis offering his portable stool to Mrs. Del Grande, who has been having hip trouble lately.

Melinda comes out of the chapel, and together with Ayler on his guitar, she leads us in the Taizé version of "Veni Sanctae Spiritus," sung in four progressive steps of harmony, sung over and over again, until it becomes a holy meditative chant. I close my eyes and let the prayerful tones of it enter and fill me, as we call the Holy Spirit down.

Father sets the tone with his opening prayer, and then we sing another Taizé song: Bless the Lord, my soul, and bless God's holy name. Bless the Lord, my soul, who leads me into life.

Christopher Bamford, Tadea's husband, and Ethan Dufault, her brother, begin the readings with alternating stanzas from St. Thérèse's poem, "An Unpetaled Rose." As they read, my pug Oggi stands panting in front of them, huffing and puffing. Ethan's young daughter, Maeve Odile, looks down and says, "Can't you be quiet?" Ezra Elliston is trilling from his stroller, but I know we are blessed by our children and animals and all the sounds they make. Mary O'Brien is standing beside me, and I can see her struggling to keep her toddler in her arms. I whisper to her, "He's fine." Little Liam is much happier standing on his own, in his blue Chinese suit with his red silk shoes.

Betty Krainis reads, and then Anne, and Stella. Finally, as the oldest woman among us, Em puts the finishing touch on the readings. She stands and takes a deep breath and sighs. "Laura has asked me to read a very moving statement, from A Story of a Soul." Her voice is quavering, and the emotion brings tears to my eyes as she continues—"At last I have found my vocation. My vocation is love! I have found my place in the bosom of the Church and it is you, Lord, who has given it to me. In the heart of the Church, who is my Mother, I will be love."

I move over next to Em and hold her hand, while Father speaks about the rose as a symbol of St. Thérèse—"The unfolding of the rose is almost like our life unfolding before God, and that was her prayer—that's all she wanted to do—basically, was to be for God. We gather here, all of us, friends, in the beauty of creation, to dedicate the work of many hands to the glory of God.

"I was reading some material that Laura gave me on how this chapel came to be," here he gives me a sly smile, "and there was a bit of a discussion, I guess, at the beginning, as to why a building? Why not just this *chapel?" He gestures to the trees above. "But Laura desired a place where you could go into, in a sense—into the womb—a quiet, safe place, and then to be able to go out and walk amidst creation. So that's what we're about—we walk in the world and yet the Creator calls us to dwell within. We walk throughout the world and see God's presence, but we also recognize the Divine spark within, the tabernacle that is our own soul."*

Father and I enter the chapel together. We light the rest of the candles, until the small space is filled with light. I pick up the two full baskets of rose petals and call out to Anyela and Grace, who then pass handfuls of fragrant petals to everyone. "What are we going to do with them?" one child asks.

"Talk about rose petals," I hear my father say. "Very appropriate for a Rose Chapel." Tadea's name is whispered. More than one person lifts the petals to her face to succumb to the perfume of the bright pink rugosas.

With an almost athletic quality, Father circles the chapel with his censer swinging incense up in all directions. I remember Tadea telling me how Father Russo had the manner of a football coach, but how much she liked him. He then takes his aspergillum and sprays holy water on the roof of the chapel. I admire the strength of his gestures.

"Now, I guess all the little ones can come right in here, all the children," he says, and they gather before him. One baby cries, and Father Russo tells him, "But you need this," smiling. He has a special fondness for children. As they stand before him, he prays over them: "Lord God, you call upon us to suffer the little children to come unto you. We ask you to bless these little ones, and those who care for them. May they be nurtured in understanding and a love of all you call into creation. May they ever keep you in their hearts. We ask this in Christ the Lord. Amen." And then he takes his little whisk broom and says—"You knew this was coming!" and he sprays them all with holy water.

Everyone is invited to make a circle around the chapel. "Bring the rose petals with you," Father shouts, and then together we toss them up on the slate roof of the chapel—a flutter of petals falls down on all sides, making a bright pink circle on the ground. Joining hands, we sing "The Lord's Prayer" before Vikki True finishes with "Amazing Grace."

As she sings this familiar, haunting song from within the stone walls of the chapel, it's as if she is singing from some distant mountain, and the chills rush through me. I feel as if her voice is anointing the very stones, anointing us all. We join in on the last refrain before she comes forward to the chapel door to sing a Celtic benediction with her big, beautiful voice—"May the road rise to meet you, and may the sun be at your back, and may the good Lord hold you ever in the palm of his hand." *Still circling the chapel, we close with a round of "Jubilate Deo" sung in a three-part round, and then everyone is invited to take turns visiting inside.*

Back on the deck the children are already helping themselves to food—a glorious abundance. Vikki True comes up to me with tears in her eyes, saying how wonderful it was to sing inside the chapel, how it was just what she needed. "Can I come back?" she asks. Mason wonders if the deck can support so many people. There are more than a hundred. Georgene, with baby Ella in an African sling, presents us with a beautiful bell. Father Russo rings it to announce that this is Ernie and Faye's fifty-fifth wedding anniversary. We raise our glasses, but where is Faye? Inside checking the dessert table.

While the guests eat, I take little Liam and my four-year-old goddaughter, Avia Rose, out to the chapel to check on the candles we left burning. We make our way out through the birch trees, and inside the chapel we close the heavy door. Silence settles.

Liam blows when I show him how to blow, though we leave a few of the votive candles burning. Avia wanders around by the colorful window, saying, "Will you come to my house, soon?" She has given me her own little bouquet of red roses. I sense that the children feel comfortable here, and I also feel content with them, away from it all.

Father Peter finally comes out to find us, and says that some of my guests are looking for me to say goodnight. As we wander back, I hear the saw-song of bullfrogs down by the pond—a tincture of fireflies dabs the darkening fields. As the full June moon now rises, I can imagine little chapels all across the country celebrating with us tonight, flickering their candles and ringing their tiny bells. Children cluster by the swing beneath the giant oak tree. They are spinning, spinning, as the earth rolls around, and yet all is still inside me, this evening as ephemeral as the smell of beeswax and incense rising—the smoke of it curling—as these rose petals fall.

Acknowledgments

I would like to give my very special thanks to Jill Johnson for her editing advice and loving support, and to the many helpful friends who have guided me along the way, especially Anne Fredericks, Anna Burgard, George and Fonda Gurtner, Barbara Brennan, Tom Howell, Bernice Abrahamzon, Rabbi Arnold Belzer, Bertrand, and Steve Gubler, as well as the loving community of friends at St. Bridget's Church in Copake Falls, New York.

My gratitude extends to Maria Hettinga, Jonathan Diamond, and Chris Tomasino, who recognized the value of the manuscript in progress, and helped move it out into the world.

My most grateful thanks go to director John Gallman as well as to our wonderful sponsoring editor, Robert Sloan, at Indiana University Press, for taking this leap of faith with us. And behind the scenes, additional thanks go to Sue Havlish, Jane Lyle, Carol A. Kennedy, and Matt Williamson.

Also to my darling boys Clovis and Ayler—may this book inspire you to find your own path; and finally to my husband, Mason Rose, the quiet force behind the creation of *Little Rose Chapel* and the sustaining presence in my life.

Notes of Credit

In the chapter about Crestone, Colorado, the quotation from William Thompson's article "The Lindisfarne Chapel" was taken from *Lindisfarne* magazine, no. 12, pages 7–8, published by the Lindisfarne Association, Copyright ©1981 by Lindisfarne Press.

The quote from Otto Rigan is from his book *From the Earth Up,* Copyright ©1979 by Otto B. Rigan, published by McGraw-Hill Book Company, 1221 Avenue of the Americas, New York, NY 10020, published in association with the San Francisco Book Company.

"Atonement for the Collective People" was excerpted from Michael Lerner's "Taking Spiritual Transformation Seriously: High Holiday Supplement 5759," *Tikkun* 13 (5), September/October 1998. *Tikkun* magazine is a bi-monthly Jewish critique of politics, culture, and society, edited by Rabbi Michael Lerner, San Francisco, California. The excerpt is reprinted with his permission. Magazine@tikkun.org.

Excerpts from *To Hear Thoroughly: Father Dunstan Morrissey Talks about His Life,* edited by Susan Moon, are reprinted with the author's and editor's permission. Copies are available from: Open Books, 1631 Grant St., Berkeley CA. 94703, ©1998 by Dunstan Morrissey. $7 per copy including shipping and handling.

The excerpt from *The Way of the Shaman,* Copyright © 1980, 1990 by Michael Harner, published by HarperSanFrancisco, is reprinted with permission from the publisher.

Two short films by Mark Elliott, *The Bloodless Valley* and *The Eye of the Land,* helped to inform the Crestone chapter. Available through *Manitou Foundation.*

The film about Jerry Wennstrom's life and work, *In the Hands of Alchemy: A Journey Through the Sacred,* was directed by Phil Lucas and Mark Sadan.

Selected Bibliography

Barrie, Thomas. *Spiritual Path, Sacred Place: Myth, Ritual and Meaning in Architecture.* Boston: Shambhala, 1996.

Boynton, Winifred C. *Faith Builds a Chapel: The Story of an Adventure in Craftsmanship.* New York: Reinhold, 1953.

Burba, Nora, and Paula Panich. *The Desert Southwest: American Design.* Photographs by Terrence Moore. New York: Bantam Books, 1987.

Cash, Marie Romero. *Built of Earth and Song: Churches of Northern New Mexico.* Santa Fe: Red Crane Books, 1993.

————. *Living Shrines: Home Altars of Mexico.* Photographs by Siegfried Halus. Santa Fe: Museum of New Mexico Press, 1999.

Cousens, Gabriel. *Sevenfold Peace.* Tiburon, Calif.: H. J. Kramer, 1990.

Descouvemont, Pierre. *Thérèse and Lisieux.* Photographs by Helmuth Nils Loose. Toronto: Novalis Press, 1996.

Drain, Thomas A. *A Sense of Mission: Historic Churches of the Southwest.* Photographs by David Wakely, with a foreword by Scott Momaday. San Francisco: Chronicle Books, 1994.

Frank, Larry. *New Kingdom of the Saints: Religious Arts of New Mexico, 1780–1907.* Santa Fe: Red Crane Books, 1992.

Gurvis, Sandra. *Way Stations to Heaven: Fifty Sites All across America Where You Can Experience the Miraculous.* New York: Macmillan, 1996.

Gutierrez, Ramon A., et al. *Home Altars of Mexico.* Photographs by Dana Salvo. Albuquerque: University of New Mexico Press, 1997.

Hall, Douglas Kent. *Frontier Spirit: Early Churches of the Southwest.* New York: Abbeville Press, 1990.

Harner, Michael. *The Way of the Shaman.* San Francisco: HarperSanFrancisco, 1980, 1990.

Heinze, Ruth-Inge. *Shamans of the Twentieth Century.* New York: Irvington, 1991.

Lawlor, Robert. *Sacred Geometry: Philosophy and Practice.* London: Thames and Hudson, 1982.

Lawlor, Robert. *The Temple in the House: Finding the Sacred in Everyday Architecture.* New York: G. P. Putnam's Sons, 1994.

Madden, Chris Casson. *A Room of Her Own: Women's Personal Spaces.* New York: C. Potter, 1997.

Mann, A. T. *Sacred Architecture.* Rockport, Mass.: Element Books, 1993.

McMann, Jean. *Altars and Icons.* San Francisco: Chronicle Books, 1998.

Miller, Mary. *Cumberland Island: The Unsung Northend.* Darien, Ga.: The Darien News, 1990.

Morrissey, Dunstan. *To Hear Thoroughly: Father Dunstan Morrissey Talks about His Life.* Edited by Susan Moon. Berkeley, Calif.: Open Books, 1998.

Pelletier, Joseph A. *The Queen of Peace Visits Medugorje.* Worcester, Mass.: Assumption Publications, 1985.

Petrisko, Thomas W. *In God's Hands: The Miraculous Story of Little Audrey Santo.* McKees Rocks, Pa.: St. Andrews Productions, 1997.

Steen, Athena Swentzell, Bill Steen, and David Bainbridge, with David Eisenberg. *The Straw Bale House.* White River Junction, Vt.: Chelsea Green Publishing Company, 1994.

Streep, Peg. *Altars Made Easy: A Complete Guide to Creating Your Own Sacred Space.* San Francisco: HarperSanFrancisco, 1997.

Sullivan, John, ed. *Experiencing Saint Thérèse Today.* Carmelite Studies no. 5. Washington, D.C.: ICS Publications, 1990.

Wallis, Michael. *En Divina Luz: The Penitente Moradas of New Mexico.* Photographs by Craig Varjabedian. Albuquerque: University of New Mexico Press, 1994.

Westwood, Jennifer. *Sacred Journeys: An Illustrated Guide to Pilgrimages around the World.* New York: Henry Holt, 1997.

Wilkens, Mike, Ken Smith, and Doug Kirby. *The New Roadside America: The Modern Traveler's Guide to the Wild and Wonderful World of America's Tourist Attractions.* New York: Simon and Schuster, 1992.

Visitor's Guide

Dear Readers,
Each family has indicated how they would like to make their private chapel available to the public. Please respect the following offerings. If a telephone number is not listed, written contact is preferred. Thank you for your respectful understanding.

William and Katina Stefanopoulos
Chapel of the Sleeping Mary, Greek Orthodox
PO Box 592, Amenia, New York 12501
914-373-8178
Directions: 1½ miles east of Amenia on Route 343.

Don Schmidt, Old Red Mill
Chapel in the Woods
Norton 2190 Hwy. K, Waupaca, Wisconsin 54981
715-258-7385
Weddings may be arranged.
Directions: Three miles south of Waupaca on Hwy. K.

Lloyd and Shirley Ferg, Ferg's Bavarian Village
St. Nicholaus Kirche
N8599 Ferg Road, Manawa, Wisconsin 54949
920-596-2946
Events: A big Christmas display, the Story of the Birth of Christ, is set up from Thanksgiving until the weekend after New Year's. Oktoberfest is the second Saturday in August.
Directions: North of Manawa on Route 22 and 110 (same road). Take a left on 161 West, go one mile to Ferg Road, and take a right—can't miss it.

Mary Anne Englebert
Belgium Shrine at Still Meadow Stables
1453 County C, Brussels, Wisconsin 54204
920-825-1337
Mary Anne is a local historian and has a sheet on the various local Belgium shrines.
Directions: North on C just outside Brussels on the left side of the road.

Our Lady of the Oaks
Directions: From Madison, Wisconsin, take Hwy. 12 heading toward Sauk City, exit Hwy. 19 West, go four miles, and Dane County Park will be on your left. It is a pleasant ten-minute hike up the hill to this charming chapel.

Bjorklunden Chapel, Scandinavian Stavkirke
Contact: Mark Breseman, Lawrence University, Bailey's Harbor, Wisconsin
920-839-2216
mark.d.breseman@lawrence.edu
Open: Mid-June through August, Mondays and Wednesdays, 1–4 P.M., groups by reservation.
Directions: Hwy. 57 North, go 4½ miles north of Jacksonport, driveway on the right, across from Anschutz Heating and Plumbing, look for signs for Lawrence University, and down the driveway follow signs for *Bjorklunden Chapel.*

Frank Lloyd Wright's Family Chapel
Unity Chapel, Taliesen
Black Earth, Wisconsin
Contact: Richard Lloyd-Jones
PO Box 82628, Portland, Oregon 97282-0628

Mr. and Mrs. Richard Dust
Corn Crib Chapel
W. 670 Joos Valley Road, Fountain City, Wisconsin 54629
608-687-8315

St. Anthony's of Padua, Smallest Cathedral in the World
Festina, Iowa
Contact: Mary Richmond
PO Box 3 Hawkeye, Iowa 52147
Directions: 5 miles southeast of Fort Atkinson, follow the signs for the smallest church, or 2½ miles southwest of Festina, on US 150.

Janet Williams
Lady Chapel, Adirondack Chapel
183 West Shore Road, Grand Isle, Lake Champlain, Vermont
802-372-3959
Open to Public: *Only* on all Sundays in August, 10:30 A.M.
Directions: Take Grand Isle Ferry to Route 314, two miles north of ferry, where there is a funny little jog in the road, continue straight on West Shore Road. Chapel entrance is the driveway after Box 183, two stone posts, on left.

Mason Rose and Laura Chester
Little Rose Chapel
PO Box 458, Great Barrington, Massachusetts 01230
Word@laurachester.com
Open: On St. Thérèse's Feast Day, October 1st.

Little Audrey's Chapel
Linda Santo
64 S. Flagg St., Worcester, Massachusetts 01615
508-755-8712
Open: Tuesday, Wednesday, and Thursday, by reservation only.
August 9, Anniversary Mass at *Christ the King Church.*

Donna DeMari, photographer
PO Box 845
Great Barrington, Massachusetts, 01230
413-528-8032

SOUTHWEST

Ettore DeGrazie Chapel
Contact: John Reyes
6300 N. Swan, Tucson, Arizona
1-800-545-2185

Capilla de San Ignacio, Straw Bale Chapel
Contact: Douglas Ruppel, Babocamari Ranch Manager
PO Box 490, Sonoita, Arizona 85637
520-455-5507

Patsy Lowry
7600 N. Moonlight Lane, Paradise Valley, Arizona 85253
480-948-6117
patsylowry@sprintmail.com

Loreto Mendez and Earl Niichel
White Dove of the Mesa, Rosicrucian Temple
HCR 2, Box 270, Mowry, Arizona, 85624
Whisperingrose@theriver.com
Overnight accommodations available. Please write for directions.

Gabriel Cousens
Essene Temple, Tree of Life Rejuvenation Center
PO Box 1080, Patagonia, Arizona 85624
520-394-2520
Directions: Take the Harshaw Road out of Patagonia. About one mile from the post office, the Tree of Life will be on the right.

Valer and Josiah Austin
El Coronado Ranch Chapel
Star Rt. 395, Pearce, Arizona 85625
520-824-3566

José and Eduvijes Gomez Gallegos
Capilla Jesús el Nazareño
PO Box 33
La Mesilla, New Mexico 88046
505-647-8720
Directions: Off Hwy. 28, 2630 Calle de Santiago

Ramon Lopez, *santero*
c/o *Good Hands Gallery*
700 Paseo de Peralta
Santa Fe, New Mexico 87501
505-982-3352

Sophia and Manuel Gurule, *santero*
44 Calle Enrique #A
Santa Fe, New Mexico 87501-0146
505-471-0859

Joan Halifax
Upaya, a Buddhist Center for personal and group retreats.
1404 Cerro Gordo Road, Santa Fe, New Mexico 87501
505-986-8518
email: upaya@rt66.com, www.peacemakercommunity.org/upaya

Lopez Family
Capilla de San Isidro
near: 1147 Cerro Gordo Road
Santa Fe, New Mexico 87501
New Mexico Historical Society Plaque
Directions: Take Palace Avenue, onto Cerro Gordo. The stone chapel will be on the left.

David Ortega
Oratorio de San Buenaventura de Plaza de Cerro de Chimayó
Ortega's Weaving Shop
PO Box 325, Chimayó, New Mexico 87522
505-351-4215
Directions: Plaza de Cerro, Intersection of County 98 and State Road 76.

Genara Chavez
Capilla de Santo Niño de Prague
Chimayó, New Mexico 87522
505-351-4729

Mickie Medina, Martinez Chapel
Capillita de Santa Rita
HC 64 Box 6-A, Chimayó, New Mexico 87522
505-351-4256
Directions: From State Road 76, take County Road 1431 on the left—you can see the tiny

chapel on top of a small hill as you drive toward Chimayó. If you can see the chapel from the road, you have missed the left-hand turn.

Zoraida and Eulogio Ortega, *santeros*
Our Lady of Guadalupe Chapel
Box 7, Velarde, New Mexico 87582
505-852-2290

John Johnson and David Heath
Windows in the Earth, The Sandstone Cathedral
Rancho de San Juan, Ojo Caliente, New Mexico
505-753-6818
Entrance Fee: $5
Accommodations available here and at Ojo Caliente Mineral Springs: 1-800-222-9162.
Directions: In Espanola take Riverside Road; left on Fairview; first right on Paseo Onate; 6 miles north, take a right at the Chevron Station, Junction 285, take a right and go about five minutes, entrance sign on right.

Rick Finney and Jerry Walter
PO Box 1853, Ranchos de Taos, New Mexico 87557
505-751-0723
rjfinter@newmex.com

SOUTH

Margaret and Hermon Dennis
All Is Welcome Temple
4535 N. Washington Street, Vicksburg, Mississippi 39183-9498
601-638-1163
Directions: 6 miles north out of Vicksburg on Washington Street, left-hand side of road.

Tezcuco Plantation Chapel
3138 Hwy. 44, Darrow, Louisiana
Accommodations available.
225-562-3929

Cheryl and Barras Cloudet
306 River Oaks, Destrehan, Louisiana 70047
504-764-9095
First Friday Rosary Group.

Kay and Hubie Mule, Mule's Religious and Office Supply
The Silver Chapel
"The Medjugorje Star"—newsletter
2627 David Drive, Metarie, Louisiana 70003
504-889-1708

Martha and Bobby DeRoche
Our Lady of Blind River, Bayou Chapel
PO Box 205, Grammercy, Louisiana 70052
Contact: Daughter Pat: 225-869-5780
Transportation to *Our Lady of Blind River* from St. James Landing on Hwy. 61.

Mr. and Mrs. Anthony J. Roppolo
The Madonna Chapel
28160 Hwy. 405, Plaquemine, Louisiana 70764
225-545-3415
Directions: From White Castle, go past Nottaway Plantation, continue for four miles, and the chapel will be on your left.

Mrs. Marion Pugh
Queen of the Most Holy Rosary Chapel
1600 Southeast Railroad Ave., Pontchatoula, Louisiana 70454
504-386-8656
Directions: Take first exit for Pontchatoula, Hwy. 51 South, go one mile.

Alfredo Raimondo
Chapel of the Holy Family and holy park
PO Box 97, Antioch Road, Tickfaw, Louisiana 70466
504-542-7537
Directions: Hwy. 61, right on 55, at Tickfaw turn left, go ½ mile and take a right on Antioch.

Annie Liuzza
Mother of Perpetual Help
12400 Liuzza Lane, Amite, Louisiana 70422
504-748-9787
Directions: From Interstate 51, take Independence exit, first red light turn left on Old Independence Hwy., between Independence and Amite.

Noonie Smith
Memorial Chapel
Hwy. 1 South, Golden Meadow, Louisiana 70416
Directions: Go through Golden Meadow, Louisiana, see chapel on left.

Priestess Miriam
Voodoo Spiritual Temple
828 N. Rampart St., New Orleans, Louisiana 70416
504-522-9627
Readings by appointment.

Retha Brannon and Lemuel Morrison
Yancy Chapel
PO Box 37, Sawyerville, Louisiana 36776
Please write for directions.

Blount Chapel
Contact: Shirley Milligan, executive assistant to Mr. Blount
4520 Executive Park Ave., Montgomery, Alabama 36116-1602
334-244-4354

Effie Grey Young
Christ's Memory Chapel
Rt. 3 Box 3163-B23, Townsend, Georgia 31331
912-832-5261
Directions: Coming from Savannah, take Hwy. 95, exit 12, take a left and go across a little bridge; before red brick Baptist church you will see a sign for smallest church in America, and you can see the chapel from there.

Faith Chapel
Jekyll Island Club, Jekyll Island, Georgia
Accommodations available.
Open: 2–4 P.M. every day unless there is a wedding.
1-800-535-9547
Directions: From Interstate 95, exit 6, onto Hwy. 17 north, go 10 miles, see sign for Jekyll Island; take causeway ($3), look for signs for the historic district.

First African Black Baptist Chapel
JFK Jr. wedding chapel
Accommodations at the Greyfield Inn, Cumberland Island, Georgia.
Reservations: 904-261-6408.

Mrs. Jim Reed
Thorncrown
Fay Jones, Architect
Eureka Springs, Arkansas
501-253-7401
Directions: Hwy. 62 west.

Howard Switzer
The Well, Penul Ridge Retreat Center
1713 15th Ave. South, Nashville, Tennessee 37212
615-383-4793

Sea Ranch Chapel
Sea Ranch Association
707-785-2444
Open: 9–5.
Accommodations available at the Sea Ranch Lodge.
Directions: Hwy. 101 North to Petaluma, Washington St. exit, left over the overpass, Bodega Hwy. (1 hour and 15 minutes from Bodega Bay to Lodge). Take Hwy. 1 north.
The chapel is 5–6 miles north of Lodge on the right-hand side, just after the fire station.

Dunstan Morrissey, Sky Farm
Chapel of the Son of Man
Please write (no phone calls)
16321 Norrbom Road, Sonoma, California 95476-0200
Retreat rooms available.

Shelley Masters
Mother Goddess Altar
415-695-7844

Edie Hartshorne, musician
Classical Japanese Tea House
Offering tea, healing water, and music.
Kyoto in Berkeley, California.
Ehartshorne@igc.org
510-526-4476

Barbara and William Howell
Sanctuary House
PO Box 332, Crestone, Colorado 81131-0332
719-256-4420
www.sanctuaryhouse.org
Sanctuary House, which can accommodate short-term and long-term retreatants on guided
and independent retreats, exists solely by donation.

Hanne and Maurice Strong
Manitou Foundation
PO Box 118, Crestone, Colorado 81131
719-256-4267
Crestone Mountain Zen Center—719-256-4692 (retreat rooms available)
Haidakhandi Universal Ashram—719-256-4108
SLV Tibetan Project—719-256-4694
The Spiritual Life Institute (Carmelites)—719-256-4778 (retreat available).

Kate Strasberg
Healing Environments
451 Lytton Ave., Palo Alto, California 94301
650-322-1428

David Tresemer
StarHouse, All Seasons Chalice
PO Box 2180, Boulder, Colorado 80306
303-245-8452
ascpr@dim.com
www.starhouse-asc.org
Solstice, Equinox, New Moon Healing Rituals.

Toni Valdez
San Francisco de Assisi Chapel
212 Gerard Avenue, Pueblo, Colorado
719-947-3723

Meditation Point Chapel
Hwy. 89, Immigrant, Montana
Directions: 32.6 miles south of Livingston, near rest stop.

Jerry Wennstrom and Marilyn Strong
Flaming Stupa Tower, Whidbey Island, Puget Sound, Washington
PO Box 522, Clinton, Washington 98236
Email: marilyn@kocreate.com
Seminar space available for individual or group retreats, with accommodations for up to fifteen people. Jungian-based counseling, spiritual direction, and dream work. Weddings and other rites of passage.

Laura Chester has been writing, editing, and publishing poetry, fiction, and non-fiction since the early 1970s. Her most recent books include a novel, *Kingdom Come* (Creative Arts Book Company); a chapbook of prose-poems, *All in All* (Quale Press*,* a new edition of *Lupus Novice,* an account of her personal struggle and breakthrough with the auto-immune disease S.L.E. (Station Hill Press); a short-story collection, *Bitches Ride Alone* (Black Sparrow Press); and a family saga, *The Story of the Lake* (Faber and Faber). She has edited several important anthologies: *Rising Tides, Deep Down, Cradle and All,* and most recently *The Unmade Bed.* Chester grew up in the Milwaukee area, and now lives with her husband in western Massachusetts.

For fourteen years **Donna DeMari** moved between Paris, Milan, and London, working as a fashion photographer. She was the first and only woman photographer to shoot for the *Sports Illustrated* swimsuit edition, in both 1994 and 1995. She has appeared on an ABC Special, shooting in Bali and Hong Kong, as well as on a "Fashion Television" segment for VH1, which highlighted her views and work as a woman photographer. Her most recent exhibition of photographs, "Horse Show," was at the SAS Gallery. She is currently working on a book of photographs, *Flying Mane.*